BALLS!

THE ALTERNATIVE FOOTBALL ANNUAL

BALLS!

SIMON BURNTON
and
ROB BAGCHI

HarperSport
An Imprint of HarperCollinsPublishers

First published in UK in 2006 by
HarperSport
an imprint of HarperCollins*Publishers*
London

© Simon Burnton and Rob Bagchi 2006

2 4 6 8 9 7 5 3 1

A CIP catalogue record for this book
is available from the British Library

ISBN-13 978-0-00-722891-1
ISBN-10 0-00-722891-0

Design by Tony Lyons

Photographs courtesy of Empics and Rex Features

Printed and bound in Great Britain by
Butler and Tanner, Frome

The HarperCollins website address is
www.harpercollins.co.uk

Disclaimer:
Balls! is a humorous publication dedicated to moderate
satire, parody and lampooning of professional football,
footballers, managers, coaches, administrators and other
sports officials. Any factual information has been sourced
from reliable media sources, which have been verified by
the authors.

CONTENTS

INTRODUCTION

It's hard to feel confident about a football-related purchase. There's no problem spotting what's really rubbish, but then a lot of what appears truly exciting and genuinely wonderful turns out to be useless once you get it home. Just look at Fernando Morientes.

Welcome to *Balls!* We'd like to think it's a guaranteed winner and, unlike Liverpool's former Spanish striker, at least it didn't cost you £6.3 million. Not, that is, unless you bought 630,000 copies, in which case thank you.

Our job is straightforward, but never simple: to hold a giant mirror up to the world of football, to take an accurate picture of what we see and then distort it slightly before putting it in a book. You might read an absurd titbit of trivia in a newspaper before immediately forgetting what it was; we write it down. You see a squirrel running across a pitch and think no more of it; we set our team of investigators on the case to find out why it was there, and when they fail we make something up.

Everything you really need to know about the 2005-06 season, about the World Cup that followed it and about the state of the game today is contained within these pages. No ifs, and definitely no butts. It's a title-winning package, offering strength in depth – about 160 pages of depth, in this case. We'd like to think there are a few star performers although you, the reader, are the boss and we'll allow you to choose which they are. We will also, if you insist, call you "gaffer".

Football is a game that seems simple but offers surprising depth to the discerning fan. *Balls!* is exactly the same. It's easy enough to navigate around – you'll notice a section on each month of last season, and one on the World Cup – but there is plenty of other stuff going on that might distract you at any moment. Our aim is to give you, and your entire family, many hours of entertainment and satisfaction.

Like your favourite player, *Balls!* is eye-catching and exciting. Like a top manager, we demand respect but don't always deserve it. Like a referee, we are independent and incorruptible. And unlike the entire Juventus squad at the first sign of trouble, we're here to stay. Until next year, then, enjoy.

Simon Burnton & Rob Bagchi
August 2006

AUGUST

Jose Mourinho releases the coat that threatened to become more famous than him, raising £22,000 for charity. He challenges "Armani, Zegna, Boss, whoever" to come up with a new version "although I must feel comfortable in it" … Darlington fan Reg Burnett, 101, is given a free season ticket in recognition of his devotion to the club and reveals he's been a fan for 60 years. The glory-seeker refuses to say who he supported for the first 40 years of his life … Chelsea's mascot, Stamford the Lion, is abducted. His head eventually turns up in Watford … Graham Poll is "fingered" in a "booze shame" probe, having, allegedly, been dragged off a car bonnet after a post fitness session piss-up. "Boys will be boys," says a Holiday Inn receptionist … Sunderland players announce a new code of conduct in which pre-massage nudity will cost them £30 … Graeme Souness defends Jermaine Jenas's transfer request by sympathising with his need to get out of "the goldfish bowl" … Frank Lampard says that despite Shaun Wright-Phillips's shyness he must still go through the Chelsea initiation ritual. Surprisingly this doesn't involve a cash-haemorrhaging trip to a Surrey bookmakers – he only has to sing a song … Neil Warnock claims that the way he works will kill him, thus saving referees the bother … Rio Ferdinand signs a new contract and thanks, in this order, "my agent, my family and the club" … Coleen McLoughlin orders a £3,000 heraldic crest with "a Chloe bag and a packet of Maltesers" to reflect her love of shopping and her sweet tooth. All satirists receive their P45s as a consequence … Laurent Robert has learnt his Newcastle lesson well and casts for early votes as Pompey's most popular dressing room figure by announcing "Here all the free-kicks are mine and the penalties too" … The Essien saga rolls on with Lyon's president, Jean-Michael Aulas, accusing Chelsea of treating him "like a narrow-minded Frenchman with a beret and a baguette" … Zinedine Zidane claims an apparition appeared to him in the middle of the night to persuade him to make his comeback for France … Southampton appoint Simon Clifford as coach … Christian Dailly trumpets himself as "the only festival going footballer" after his trip to Glastonbury and reveals he has his own band. Sadly he suggests that "none of the lads would understand our music" (so it's not a Tina Turner tribute act then) ... When Wigan took on Chelsea on the first day of the season, their team cost a total of £7.625m. Chelsea's cost £120m ... Dundee United's David Fernandez finally earns comparisons with Beckham, though it's not for his pinpoint set-pieces – he needed three stitches after being hit in the head by manager Gordon Chisholm's shoe ... Alan Smith turned down an England call-up to play (and score) for Manchester United's reserves against Bolton ... Permanently furious goalkeeper Oliver Kahn was leading a campaign in Germany for a new version of *Football's Coming Home* to be recorded before the World Cup ... Seth Johnson returned to Derby, bringing to an end an unhappy if lucrative spell at Leeds. "I have had enough of sunbathing and lying on a beach," he said. "I hate that." Don't we all ... Unlike Johnson, the England team were still dreaming of beaches when being beaten 4-1 by Denmark. "The way we came out in the second half was like we were on holiday," said Sven-Goran Eriksson ... David James admitted that he wasn't fully prepared for his shambolic second-half appearance in that game. "There were things I did which I will make totally sure I never do again," he said ... A fee of almost £25m takes Michael Essien to Chelsea. "I know what I'm worth at a playing level, and it's clear I'm not worth £24.4m," he says ... The Glazers pay an "adviser" to sit with them at matches to explain tactics and interpret fans' chants ... Milan Baros signed for Villa after revealing their enterprising negotiation techniques: "At the first meeting I told them my ideas about the amount I wanted," he said. "And they increased it." ... Freddie Ljungberg's bedroom techniques got a public airing. "Freddie is very, very kinky when it comes to sex – and I love that," said the model Madeleine Lexander, recently voted Sweden's fourth sexiest woman. "What an amazing lover." A spokesman for the Arsenal midfielder denied their relationship ... Clive Oliver, 43, refereed Rotherham's Carling Cup match against Port Vale. One of his assistants was his 20-year-old son Michael ... Frank Lampard's fiancée Elen Rivas gave birth to their first child by caesarean section, timed to coincide with a visit from her 93-year-old Spanish grandmother ... Sven and his partner Nancy Dell'Olio booked into the Grove hotel in Hertforshire under the name Mr and Mrs Eric Jones ... Hartlepool's Adam Boyd fled down the street wearing just a t-shirt after being caught in bed with a woman by her ex-boyfriend ... Pope Benedict XVI meets Pele and has to ask an aide who the greatest footballer ever is ... Christian Bassila was convinced to sign for Sunderland because of Mick McCarthy's French, picked up during a short spell at Lyon. "My Lyon team-mates used to tell me I spoke French like a Spanish cow," the manager says ...

Managers of the month
AUGUST
Who won the awards:

PREMIERSHIP

Stuart Pearce (Man City)
Three wins and a draw from City's first four games is pretty good going, although slightly less impressive when you realise that those wins came against Birmingham, Sunderland and Portsmouth.

CHAMPIONSHIP

Neil Warnock (Sheffield United)
Five wins and one defeat from six league games is a fine start to the campaign.

LEAGUE ONE

Peter Jackson (Huddersfield Town)
Lost to Nottingham Forest on the first day of the season, but came back with four wins and a draw from their remaining August fixtures.

LEAGUE TWO

Gudjon Thordarson (Notts County)
Four wins and two draws from six games.

Who should have won the award:

Gordon Chisholm (Dundee United)
Admittedly not strictly speaking eligible for a manager of the month award in England, he gets the vote for his superior man-handling skills and besides, it's probably the only award he's going to get – he was sacked in January. Angry about a refereeing decision that went against him, Chisholm kicked a nearby water bottle, dislodging his shoe which flew into the air and landed in the face of newly-signed striker David Fernandez, who was preparing to come on as substitute. "There's no problem between us, but it's not the best way to kick off our working relationship," said our far from strait-laced hero after the 3-0 defeat to Hearts. Fernandez required stitches. It's not known how Chisholm responded to his sacking.

Fired!

Er, nobody (although Millwall's **Steve Claridge** managed a season-busting July departure). Don't worry, they make up for it in September.

STATISTICS

Top scorers

Geoff Horsfield (West Brom) – 4
Darren Bent (Charlton) – 4
Ruud van Nistelrooy
     (Manchester United) – 3
Thierry Henry (Arsenal) – 3
Didier Drogba (Chelsea) – 2

So far this season

Most corners: **Blackburn** – 32
Most fouls: **Blackburn** – 72
Shots off target: **Bolton** – 29
Shots per goal: **Liverpool** – 31
Hit the woodwork: **Charlton/Villa** – 3

Match of the month
WIGAN 0 CHELSEA 1

In which we discovered five things: 1) Wigan might just be better than we thought; 2) Chelsea aren't really that good, at least not all the time; 3) Even when Chelsea aren't that good they still win 4) Pascal Chimbonda thinks it's so cold he's got to wear gloves in summertime. You might have expected the issue of Chimbonda's gloves to dominate post-match discussion, but the managers tiresomely talked about the game. "Wigan did not deserve to lose," said Jose Mourinho. "Normally the wake-up call is when you lose. Today we had a wake-up call without losing any points."

Top of the table

		P	W	D	L	F	A	GD	Pts
1	CHELSEA	4	4	0	0	8	0	8	12
2	MANCHESTER CITY	4	3	1	0	6	3	3	10
3	CHARLTON ATHLETIC	3	3	0	0	7	1	6	9
4	MANCHESTER UNITED	3	3	0	0	5	0	5	9
5	BOLTON WANDERERS	4	2	1	1	6	4	2	7

THE THOUGHTS OF CHAIRMAN CARLOS

CARLOS QUEIROZ'S
FOOTBALL HANDBOOK
MODULE 1 – THE ART OF DEFENCE

"BEREFT OF AN appreciation of the art of defence, the football pitch becomes a crass, hedonistic playground. The objective of defence is the promotion of the purity of a football match, a bold attempt to repel the barbarian. Defence is art; attack the populist, philistine critic. The attacker appeals to the base instinct, indulgent literal fripperies such as shots and goals are the petrol station bouquets of the game – improvised, charmless and symbolic of a gaudily nauseating desperation to please. But the horizontal pass, the incorruptible perfection of the binary scoreline and the pre-eminence of stifling above trifling are the ideals that shape the aesthetic framework of the game's infinitely more subtle abstract appeal. And so, this defensive disquisition commences with the pass back to the goalkeeper. Think of it as a homecoming, the recalcitrant ball returning to the bosom of its mother who will cherish, not chastise it. Behave like a responsible citizen and rush to the aid of a child in distress wherever you are on the football field. By all means greet it, comfort it, mollycoddle it first ... but remember it is not an orphan, its destiny yours to mould. Send it home before the savages lead it astray."

Theo's Diary

Today I was allowed to play with the grown-ups for the first time and they had a big playground much bigger than school and it was soft and had grass on it and it was dead nice and must have been famous because lots of people had come to look at it and I was really excited but the headmaster made me sit on the bench for a long time and I didn't know why but in the end he let me run around a bit and everyone was really nice.

Gordon Strachan's cheeseboard
Danish Blue

THE FRENCH BLUE-VEINED CHEESES have their fans, the Italians have class aplenty on their day when teamed with a grape but this Scandinavian mould cheese never flatters to deceive. It is functional and effective. It's always a threat in international tournaments, no matter the consistency of the curd. It's got some bite to it, it'll keep the rest of the team on their toes no problem. It also stands out from the rival Norwegian Blue, which has a good go but falls down because, unlike the more reliable cheeses, it's a fictional parrot and frequently dead.

Welcome to... Middlesbrough

In which players introduce us to the towns they live in. This month, Middlesbrough left-back Emanuel Pogatetz's thoughts on Teesside. We should add, charitably, that he later denied having said any of this. "Somebody has added new words to what I really said," he insisted. "It's ridiculous." Being intelligent folk, you can make your own mind minds up. Anyway, here it is.

"Thank God it's only on match days we have to go into Middlesbrough. The place is an industrial town, pure and simple. The club's training centre is outside the town and the players live outside it as well. I wouldn't want to live in the town – all you've got there is smoking chimneys."

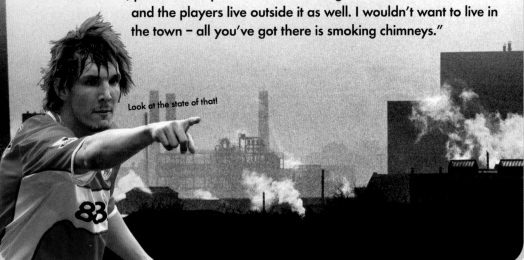

Look at the state of that!

JOSE MOURINHO'S
Dossier
✦ ✦ ✦ ✦ ✦ ✦ August 2005 ✦ ✦ ✦ ✦ ✦ ✦

JOSE'S
ARSENAL
WATCH.

Cabbage
Broccoli
Asparagus
Carrots
Sweetcorn
Sprouts
Chard
Cauliflower
Beetroot
Courgettes
Spinach
Cucumber

Lentils???

"Chelsea this, Chelsea that, Chelsea the antichrist." All summer I have had to put up with Wenger's criticism about us. First he accuses me of taking Ashley Cole to tea, next that I have paid too much for Shaun Wright-Phillips. He is a nosey parker, a fish wife who covets another fish family's catch. "Look at their haul," he carps, "he must have a very dear Russian net, far bigger than everyone else's. It is a sturgeon net, not designed for use in British waters. It is unfair. I will report his net to the authorities. They must investigate it. Anyway, it takes more skill and is infinitely more satisfying to catch a sprat with a shoelace and a pole than to sweep the ocean floor with his expensive equipment." On and on he goes, but I have had enough of his prattle. I have not been plucked from the tree with wet ear lobes. I am Jose. I am wonderful. I am fair minded. I am suave. I am a genius. I am very long-suffering. I am supremely chic. I am the world's best father I have a mug to prove it. I am spellbinding. I am fertile. I am Jose. I am tolerant, but no more.

Yes I did take tea with Cole. He devoured his cucumber sandwiches like a man whose manager is not catering to his need for botanical fruits. My players get as much salad as they want. They eat vegetables, all the time. I like them to eat plenty of stem, leaf and flower varieties. They gorge on cruciferous greens: broccoli, cauliflower, even the bitter sprouts. I said to Cole: "You come to Chelsea and the world will be your allotment. You will have the diet of a rabbit king. I do not grow them myself but if I did you would never have heard of the hairy River Cottage aristo-peasant." He smiled, he was happy. I knew then that he had the hunger to come to Chelsea. But I don't always put the best food on the menu. I rotate it on the basis of what I think is best for Chelsea. How would he feel if, instead of the vegetables he was used to, I suddenly dropped cucumbers and introduced pulses to the diet? He smiled. He was happy. I knew then that he had the versatility to come to Chelsea.

With Shaun it was the same. He knew a vegetable lover when he saw one. Wenger wears glasses, obvious proof of a carrot deficiency. "Reassuringly expensive" I think is the current expression for our players. I shop in the best places. I look in the mirror and ask myself, "Shall I buy him?" He costs a lot, yes, but I deserve it and we will continue to deserve it because we are blue with natty white socks. We wear rampant lions on our chests. We are proud. We are special.

Walter Pandiani
Birmingham City

Date of Birth: 27 April 1976 in Montevideo, Uruguay

Nickname: El Rifle – The rifle, presumably because he's off like a shot

Bought for: £3m from Deportivo La Coruna, August 2005 after six-month loan

Sold for: £1m to Espanyol, January 2006

Previous occupation: Municipal dustman, Montevideo

Likes: Bruce Lee, monster trucks, Mr Bean

Dislikes: Birmingham, La Coruna

Vehicles: Mini cooper (with Union Jack livery), Iveco Pegas (Bright red with his nickname in very large letters and two beds in the back)

Marks out of 10: Desire 8; Ability 4; Heading 3; Shooting 2; Value for money 1

Vital statistics: In Uruguay: 50 games, 29 goals, 0.58 goals per game; In Spain: 118 games, 46 goals, 0.39 goals per game; In England: 31 games, 6 goals, 0.19 goals per game.

A career in quotes

On arrival: "I'm only here because Deportivo La Coruna made this happen and my wife forced me to come . . . I wanted to go to Fiorentina but Deportivo – maybe on purpose – took time sending the fax and I am in Birmingham – just where I didn't want to be."

The next day: "What was reported was not what I actually said. The Premiership is a great competition. It's an honour to play in England and be in Birmingham."

A Deportivo "insider" adds: "Walter has a bad attitude. The English club will have to keep an eye on him or it could go wrong."

Steve Bruce's opinion: "I think this fella is the new king on the block of Birmingham. I'm sure he'll do very well for us."

Steve Bruce's opinion, four months later: "You don't just lose your ability."

David Sullivan adds: "You've got to take your hat off to his commitment to the club. He brought all his family over and bought a big house."

El Rifle concludes: "I'm glad to be back in Spain. I've got a lot of friends here."

THE HARD SELL

SCENE: A telephone line linking Newcastle to Madrid.

Alan: "Michael? It's the big man here. We want you to come home . . ."

Michael: "Crouchy! Thank God you've rung. I thought I might end up at Wigan or Everton, even Newc . . ."

Alan: "It is Newcastle, Michael. It's Alan Shearer here, not Peter Crouch like . . ."

Michael: "I think I'm going to try to force my way in here, Alan . . ."

Alan: "You should come here, Michael, you'll be a legend like. We've got so much to offer . . ."

Michael: "Yeah?"

Alan: "Yeah . . . Get Carter . . . sleeping giant . . . three FA Cups in the 1950s . . . Milburn, MacDonald, Keegan, Shearer . . . the iconic No 10 shirt worn by er Silvio Maric . . . 52,000 sell-out every fortnight . . . Bob Ferris and Terry Collier . . . the best fans in the world . . . the Angel of the North . . . you haven't really played football if you've never experienced playing in the north-east hotbed . . . crocodile shoes . . . stottie cakes . . . the Quayside . . . if you get it right up here, I tell you, there's no bigger club in the world like . . . the Venerable Bede . . . a walk on Whitley Bay sands . . . Chris Waddle's sausage factory . . . Sting . . . Billy Elliott . . . that bloke from Dire Straits . . . Hughie Gallacher . . . Jayne Middlemiss . . . Simon Smith and his dancing bear . . . Ooh Byker, Byker, Byker Grove . . ."

Michael: "Umm . . ."

Alan: "Er . . . World Cup year like . . . Wynyard . . . Jossie's Giants . . . Redcar races . . . being called Michael all the time on Match of the Day . . . day trips to Stavanger . . . you can commute from Chester . . . did I mention the best fans in the world?"

Michael: "Umm . . ."

Alan: "A hundred grand a week?"

Michael: "I'll book me flight."

AS A SPECIAL service for football managers, who have to write programme notes every other week for their entire careers and are often stuck for something to say, *Balls!* has compiled this easy-to-use template. We'd like to think it offers everything the average fan is looking for – topicality, frankness, terrible jokes, and sentences that inexplicably end in an exclamation mark!

Good **evening / afternoon** and welcome to the latest game in what is proving a **fascinating / exciting / disastrous** season. First of all, I'd like to extend a warm welcome to [**first name**] [**surname**] and his [**team name**] team. I first met [**surname**]ey many years ago, back in my playing days, and will always remember him as a wonderful bloke, forever with a smile on his face – though I hope he won't be wearing one come the end of **today's / tonight's** game! Seriously though, he's doing a **wonderful / difficult** job and hopefully come the end of the season – if not before – he'll be rewarded with the **promotion / knighthood / dismissal** he deserves.

[Insert photo here]

As always, there's been a lot of action around the club since the last home game. First of all, I'm **delighted / angry / slightly nonplussed** that [**first name**] [**surname**] has **signed / refused** to sign his new contract. [**Surname**]ey's never made any secret of his desire to **stay at / leave** the club, and whatever your thoughts about him you should be pleased that his wishes have come true – particularly if you happen to be his agent!

We had **better / worse** luck in last **Saturday / Sunday lunchtime / Sunday afternoon / Monday evening / Tuesday night / Wednesday's** game at [**team name**]. I don't know if you managed to make it to the match, or catch the highlights on the **BBC / ITV / Sky / a dodgy Swedish satellite channel**, but I thought we dominated it from the off and really took the game to them. I've been asking my players to deliver me performances like that and I can't have any complaints with the way they responded. The **victory / draw / defeat** was therefore **thoroughly deserved / disappointing / a bit of a shock, and / but** we hope that level of performance can be maintained as we push on for the rest of the season.

A look at the league table will tell you that we're doing **really well / badly / averagely** at the moment, and I've every confidence that we can **maintain / turn around** our current form. We made our aims for the season perfectly clear at the start of the season, and with your backing I'm sure we'll still be able to deliver the **league title / play–off spot / European place / last–minute escape from relegation / cynical asset–stripping** that the chairman demanded back in the summer.

There's been a lot of speculation about the transfer market recently, with the transfer window **about to open / just closed / still bloody miles away**. Obviously as fans you like to see top players coming to the club, and that's exactly what I like too. Sadly, the **size of the squad / league position / chairman's avarice** will limit our activity in the immediate future, but you never know – I might have a few surprises up my sleeve!

All that might be about to change, if what you might have read in the papers about the club being bought out by a **Russian oil magnate / Arab billionaire / dodgy American tycoon / shadowy consortium** turns out to be true. I'm as much in the dark about this as you are, but I certainly believe that this club has massive potential and we've all seen in the past this kind of investment has brought **enormous success / continued mediocrity / relegation and financial ruin** to **Chelsea / Portsmouth / Leeds United**. This club is every bit as big as they are, and with any luck we'll be battling against them in future months for the world's top **players / bankruptcy lawyers**.

Today marks the conclusion of **my first year as manager/the annual Kick Racism Out of Football campaign / the Senegalese elections / British Sausage Week**, so I'd like to take this opportunity to thank **my wife / the hard-working and dedicated campaigners / all those who support the battle for democracy / my butcher** for all **her / their / his** efforts. The people behind the scenes often don't get the thanks they deserve, and that's something I'd like to take this opportunity to put straight.

Finally, a few words about the pitch. It's always hard to keep the surface just right through the winter months, and I think our groundsman **[first name] [surname]** and his team have done an absolutely **fantastic / bloody awful** job of it. All the players **appreciate / detest** him for all the **hard work / hours in the pub** he puts in and I'll certainly be **backing his application for the groundsman of the year award / sending him his P45** over the next few weeks!

That's all from me. Until next time, enjoy the game!

[Sign here]

"My first..."
Lee Bowyer

what you lookin' at?

MY FIRST BREATH On 3 January when I was born in London. I was brought up in the Teviot estate in Tower Hamlets, which is well rough, and went to Langdon Park school.

MY FIRST-TEAM DEBUT In the 1994-95 season I managed to play five games for Charlton, my first taste of success.

MY FIRST GOAL The following season, 1995-96, I scored eight which was like brilliant and good enough to get me a move.

MY FIRST UNDER-21 CAP Came in May 1996. I went on to win 13.

MY FIRST BIG MOVE I became Britain's most expensive teenager when Leeds bought me from Charlton for £2.8m in 1996.

MY FIRST SENIOR ENGLAND CAP In September 2002 I started the friendly against Portugal. After 62 minutes, I was replaced by Trevor Sinclair.

MY FIRST BROKEN RECORD If you don't count that transfer fee, in 1999-2000 I became the first person to get 14 yellow cards in a Premiership season – and won a £4,000 fine which was a bit harsh, like.

MY FIRST FINE Leeds were fined £150,000 at the start of that season and it was all my fault, after my foul on Stephen Clemence prompted a brawl. A bit of an over-reaction, I reckon.

MY FIRST RUN-IN WITH THE AUTHORITIES In March 1995 I tested positive for marijuana in a random drug test. Charlton banned me for eight weeks and I was dropped by England Under-18s. "It was horrible but I'd made a mistake and I had to pay for it, didn't I?" I said.

you, ya muggy c*nt

MY FIRST INEXPLICABLE ACT OF VIOLENCE In December 1996 I was fined £4,500 after throwing chairs across a McDonald's restaurant on a night out. It wasn't that bad because a Leeds spokesman said I'd shown "true contrition". Whatever that means.

MY FIRST NATIONAL CONTROVERSY I was accused of assaulting a student but I was found not guilty of all charges in December 2001. I would be tempted to make a joke about it here but that would be in very poor taste.

MY FIRST LITTLE MOVE In January 2003 only £300,000 took me from Leeds to West Ham. Worse, at the end of the season Newcastle got me for nothing. Now I'm back at West Ham for an 'undisclosed fee'. Which is a posh way of saying 'free'.

MY FIRST ON-PITCH PUNCH-UP WITH A TEAM-MATE Strangely, this didn't come until April 2005 when I had a quick scrap with Kieron Dyer during a game against Aston Villa. I got fined six weeks' wages, which was well harsh as I was dead sorry and said so after.

MY FIRST REALLY LONG BAN In January 2003 I got six matches from Uefa for a stamp on Malaga's midfielder Gerardo, though I ended up with seven for that Kieron Dyer business.

Sausage? Chicken? Burgers ain't done yet

Which end? Oh bollocks.

SEPTEMBER

Some 20,000 Newcastle fans greet Michael Owen, who arrives carrying his two-year-old daughter Gemma – probably the only thing he'll have to parade around the St James' Park pitch for the foreseeable future ... David Ginola is voted the sexiest footballer ever in a poll of 3,000 women, followed by David Beckham. More surprising names on the list include No7 Milan Baros and, at No14, Ray Wilkins ... Jimmy Floyd Hasselbaink celebrates his first three points of the season, added to his driving license as he's caught driving at 87mph ... Dean Windass, Bradford's ageing striker, reveals why he turned down a move to Premiership Wigan: "My wife Helen is carving out a career for herself with North Yorkshire Police in Harrogate and I've become super-dad." ... Discount £1 fish and chip suppers at Fosters chippie in fashionable Cheshire town Alderley Edge attract Andy Cole and Wolves' Mark Kennedy – but they get there too late and miss out ... Diego Maradona is sued by his son Diego Jnr for psychological damage after he called his progeny a mistake ... Tunbridge Wells beat Littlehampton 16–15 on penalties in an FA Cup preliminary round replay ... It's revealed that the first thing Nolberto Solano did upon returning to Newcastle is invite everyone round for a barbeque. "He told me to bring everyone I know," said Kieron Dyer. "That's the type of lad he is." ... Goldie Lookin' Chain play before England play Wales, and dedicate *Your Missus is a Nutter* to David Beckham. Joe Cole scores the only goal in a poor performance, with Steven Gerrard playing three positions ... The FA fax high-security information on the England team, including their passport numbers, to a random Belfast business rather than the team hotel after dialling a wrong number ... Northern Ireland get their first competitive win for four years against Azerbaijan, and then beat England three days later ... Jose Mourinho makes his team do aqua aerobics to aid balance and coordination. John Terry is reported to wear "camp lime green bathers" ... Paul Robinson's house is burgled, his wife's jewellery stolen ... MK Dons commission sculptor Ernest Bottomley, 71, to make a £40,000 sculpture of Vinnie Jones squeezing Gazza's gonads ... America's Landon Donovan enjoys victory over Mexico: "They suck," he says. "Hopefully that will shut them up for the next three or four years." ... A list of the most stylish people in football puts Carlo Cudicini top and Jose Mourinho third. Interestingly, Gary Neville comes ninth ... The FA react to the Northern Ireland debacle by getting a new couch. Somewhere, a secretary is sacked for misspelling "coach" ... Anton Ferdinand and Nigel Reo-Coker are mugged outside a kebab shop, the assailants making off with Ferdinand's £10,000 Rolex, plus Ferdinand's mobile phones and gold chains. "It was a frightening experience," says a "colleague". The dastardly deed turns out to have been committed by the boyfriend of a model whose phone number young Anton had acquired earlier that evening ... It is reported that, ahead of the Northern Ireland game, David Beckham made hotel staff pick the cucumber and tomato out of a salad. Wayne Rooney, meanwhile, was banned from eating a chicken and mayonnaise sandwich ... In a conference on celebrity at Paisley University, Dr Carlton Brick presents a paper called: "Father, Why Hast Thou Forsaken Me? Post-Modernism, Desire and Dissatisfaction: A Case Study of David Beckham's Meaning". His talk is followed by a case study of the meaning of the title of the case study of David Beckham's meaning. Several attendees later expire of confusion ... Keith Curle is racially abused at a petrol station: "I'm not having a woman having a racist attitude to myself," he storms, adding fuel to the whole racism or sexism, which is worst debate ... AC Milan's team doctor Armando Gozzini is charged with indecently exposing himself to a hotel worker while having a massage in Manchester ... Wayne Rooney sent off for sarcastically applauding referee Kim Milton Neilsen against Villareal. "It saddened me to have to send him off," says the ref. Sir Alex Ferguson explains that: "Rooney's from Liverpool and everyone from that city has a chip on their shoulder" ...Rooney appears with rapper 50 Cent at the MEN Arena ... Diego Maradona appears on the Italian version of Celebrity Come Dancing ... Coleen McLoughlin is named celebrity shopper of the year ... Jonathan Woodgate finally makes his Real Madrid debut, 516 days after joining the club. He scores an own goal and is sent off ... Birmingham City set up a funeral service – you get a blue and white coffin and get your ashes scattered on the pitch. The only thing to go up in smoke at this stage in the season however is the team's hopes of Premiership survival...

SEPTEMBER

Who won the awards:

PREMIERSHIP

Paul Jewell (Wigan Athletic)

Two wins and a draw from three games is quite good in anyone's book, and considerably better than that in Wigan's book. Plus he tried to sign Dean Windass, worth a medal in itself.

CHAMPIONSHIP

Neil Warnock (Sheffield United)

Five games, five wins, one award. With a month like that, you can start clearing some space on the mantelpiece. Chris Kamara praised their "steely determination". Was that a pun, Chris?

LEAGUE ONE

Steve Tilson (Southend United)

Five games, five wins, one award. See Warnock, Neil (above). "His side are definitely making a massive impact in League One," said an obvious-stating Kamara, chairman of the panel of judges (one of their easier meetings, this one).

LEAGUE TWO

John Gorman (Wycombe Wanderers)

Two draws and three wins is a slightly dubious way to sneak into an awards ceremony if you ask us, even if Gorman's side did, by the start of October, boast the last unbeaten record in the football league. "John must take a huge amount of credit," said Kamara.

Who should have won the award:

Jose Mourinho (Chelsea)

Not, as you might have guessed, for being in charge of the Premiership leaders and eventual run-away champions – he never got a manager of the month award for that, weirdly – but for making his team do aqua aerobics. Apparently underwater star jumps and, yes, synchronised swimming were ordered to improve the side's balance and co-ordination. So Chelsea managed to do to themselves what no domestic opponent could manage all season – make them look like total idiots. But it was all for a worthwhile cause, namely improving their fitness, their balance, and their all-round athletic ability. Sadly, it didn't work on Robert Huth.

Fired!

After a nervous start to the season the nation's chairmen finally got their axes working in the season's second month, with heads rolling at an astonishing rate. On average a managerial P45 was prepared every third day in September, and here's your full list of the month's movers and shakers, including one mover from the shakers:

Bobby Williamson (Plymouth)
Brian Tinnion (Bristol City)
Carlton Palmer (Mansfield Town)
Graham Barrow (Bury)
Ian Atkins (Bristol Rovers)
Gary Johnson (Yeovil Town)
Andy King (Swindon Town)

STATISTICS

Top scorers (league only):

Darren Bent (Charlton) – 5
Ruud van Nistelrooy (Manchester United) – 5
Frank Lampard (Chelsea) – 4
Marlon Harewood (West Ham) – 4
Geoff Horsfield (West Brom) – 4

So far this season

Most corners: **Blackburn** – 44
Most fouls: **Newcastle** – 121
Shots off target: **Bolton** – 48
Shots per goal: **Everton** – 48
Hit the woodwork: **Manchester City** – 5

Match of the month
NORTHERN IRELAND 1
ENGLAND 0

In which we discovered that 1) even when fit and playing rubbish teams Wayne Rooney can be useless. He is also capable of swearing at team-mates with almost the same level of fury with which he treats referees; 2) Sven-Goran Eriksson could lose qualifiers, though not often and only against the bad teams; 3) there's no such thing as an easy fixture in international football these days. Though we probably knew that already; 4) it's all very well to chant "Sven Out" at the first sign of trouble, but if the fans going mental on the terraces knew that they might as well be singing "Steve McClaren in", they might have thought twice before getting so excited, and finally 5) isn't it funny that the media immediately stop harping on about bringing back the Home Championships when it looks like England might not win it?

Top of the table

		P	W	D	L	F	A	GD	Pts
1	CHELSEA	7	7	0	0	14	1	13	21
2	CHARLTON ATHLETIC	6	5	0	1	10	4	6	15
3	BOLTON WANDERERS	7	4	2	1	8	4	4	14
4	TOTTENHAM	7	3	3	1	6	3	3	12
5	WEST HAM UNITED	6	3	2	1	10	4	6	11

Bottom of the table

		P	W	D	L	F	A	GD	Pts
16	PORTSMOUTH	7	1	2	4	5	9	-4	5
17	FULHAM	7	1	2	4	5	10	-5	5
18	WEST BROM	7	1	2	4	7	13	-6	5
19	SUNDERLAND	7	1	1	5	5	10	-5	4
20	EVERTON	6	1	0	5	1	7	-6	3

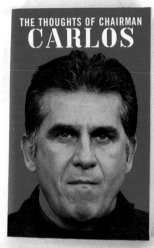

THE THOUGHTS OF CHAIRMAN CARLOS

CARLOS QUEIROZ'S
FOOTBALL HANDBOOK
MODULE 2 – PASS AND MOVE

❝ **PASS AND MOVE**, pass and move. It's the only way to win. I cannot repeat it enough. But when you sit at the very highest level of the coaching three-tier wedding cake, it is not necessary to move your entire body. If you watch the very best managers, sometimes you can notice barely a flicker as the game moves around them, yet they are still directing the action like the very finest conductor. Take Stuart Pearce, for example. He is young. He patrols the touchline like a raging bull who has been force-fed extremely powerful steroids. True, when he was a left-back you could have said the same, but you can tell that he is a young manager because of his exaggerated movements. Now, look at someone with experience, someone with gravitas, someone with the respect of the whole world of football and see how they behave. For example, me. I have been known to spend entire matches without moving more than my eyebrow. This may explain Rio Ferdinand's unusual positioning in some games, but he will learn to read each hair on my brow, given time. It is enough. The point is made. Pass and move. ❞

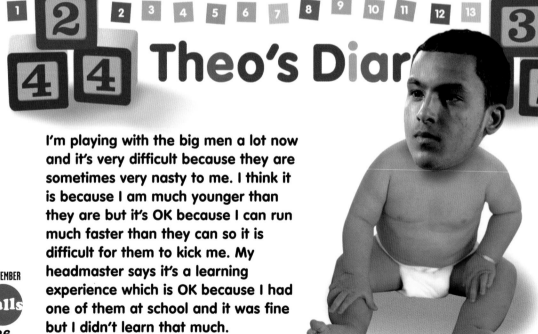

Theo's Diary

I'm playing with the big men a lot now and it's very difficult because they are sometimes very nasty to me. I think it is because I am much younger than they are but it's OK because I can run much faster than they can so it is difficult for them to kick me. My headmaster says it's a learning experience which is OK because I had one of them at school and it was fine but I didn't learn that much.

Gordon Strachan's cheeseboard
Dolcelatte

SOMETIMES A CHEESE might look a bit fatty and useless but you'll find it's got hidden bite, and this is one of those. To look at it, it wouldn't be much of a challenge – while it was quite firm when it was young, when it matures a bit it starts oozing at the edges. Kind of like Paul Merson. But it's what's inside that counts and when you get behind that pallid, clammy skin you find that boy has meanness running through its veins.

Welcome to... Liverpool

Spanish midfielder Luis Garcia loves most things about England, except the social timetables, the weather and the language. In other words, it's much worse than Spain. "In Barcelona or Madrid you can go out more and enjoy the street life because of the sunny weather and the café lifestyle. But here there's no one left on the streets after 6pm," he said. As for the language, "I brought my dog to Liverpool and he was able to speak Scouse in two days. But I still can't."

Arr, eh la', come 'ead...

¿Que?

Nightclubs

THERE IS A GOOD FOOD GUIDE. There is a good hotel guide. But what do you do when you need a hot nightspot? And what, or who, defines heat anyway?

We do, that's who. Or rather our footballers do, but we filter their activities like a big paper kaleidoscope. We've been keeping our beady eye on the nation's tabloids for rather longer than is strictly healthy, and from them we've fashioned this handy guide to where Britain's top stars go when they need to let their hair down.

You may very well have thought that, being professional athletes who are engaged in an extremely rigorous season from August until May every year, with rather strenuous pre-season training occupying much of July and the World Cup / European Championships / expensive holidays in Dubai with June, there really wouldn't be much time for extensive hair-letting. But you'd be wrong.

Footballers, you see, are young, fit and healthy. They can, it seems, go out until four in the morning and still turn up for training the next day and convince everyone that they spent the previous evening at home watching *Finding Nemo* on DVD. They can recover very quickly from almost all ailments, except of course broken metatarsals. Fortunately a hangover can be dealt with in a matter of hours, while a sordid sexual liaison in a nightclub toilet is less troublesome still, at least until the details appear in a tabloid newspaper and you have to explain the situation to your faithful fiancée.

So many stories fill the papers that it is tempting to look at these people as professional socialites who play football for a hobby. But despite the evidence, the players themselves continue to insist that a night out is a rare treat, that there is no drinking culture, that they're just quiet, well-behaved boys really. "The whole drinking culture has gone out of the window because if you do it too much it is going to show," says Jermaine Jenas. "A quiet drink is okay now and again, but don't go silly and be doing it week in, week out."

So here are some of the places where British footballers go for "a quiet drink" "now and again".

Use these handy icons to see what they get up to and where...

CELEBRATIONS   FASHION   £ MONEY   LOVE & ROMANCE   SWEARING   WOMEN

CONTROVERSY   FIGHTS   MUSIC   SMOKING   TOILET-BASED ANTICS   FOOD

COURT CASES   ICE CUBES   PAPARAZZI   UNLIKELY COUPLES   TRAVEL   ALCOHOL

CHINAWHITE, LONDON

6 Air Street W1B 5AA
Telephone: 020 7343 0040
www.chinawhite.com

Promises to fuse "the oriental styles of Bali, Java and Sumatra" with "a theatrical flair that owes much to the influence of ballet, theatre and film sets" to create an environment in which Jodie Marsh will feel at home - an almost impossible combination, you'd have thought. They have a famously strict door policy, which basically means that unless you're exceptionally wealthy or mind-bogglingly beautiful you're not getting in.

Tabloid tales

Fans/stalkers of Chelsea, Spurs and the boy-band Blue should head straight here. This, after all, is where John Terry, after a night out with Wayne Bridge, Frank Lampard, Glen Johnson and Joe Cole, started an affair with the extraordinarily-named Shalimar Wimble who, on an entirely separate occasion, was seen here swapping numbers with Eidur Gudjohnsen while wearing "the tiniest of tops". Then there was William Gallas, spotted "smooching" topless model Samantha Nelemans last December before leaving in a taxi at 4.30am. "Sam was clearly smitten," said a "partygoer". Didier Drogba was seen kissing glamour model Alicia Douvall here as he celebrated last season's Community Shield victory. So that's pretty much the whole Chelsea team covered. In other news, Ashley Cole spent an evening here with Jermaine Jenas, Jermain Defoe, Kieran Richardson and Joe Cole which ended with him almost getting in a fight with a group of men who were teasing him about being tapped up by Chelsea. "He looked the worse for wear and got quite angry," said "one witness".

BROWNS, LONDON

4 Great Queens St WC2 / Tel.020 7831 0802

General consensus is that Browns isn't what it once was. The uber-trendy crowd has moved elsewhere, but a few slow-on-the-uptake footballers are still turning up for some fluorescent-dancefloor-based fun.

Tabloid tales

Another Chelsea hangout, their former full-back Celestine Babayaro was once seen partying here with model Cassie Sumner, before taking her back to his flat where his bed "has black satin sheets and is covered in black fur". She went on to describe how they "ripped each other's clothes off" before something "like an explosion" occurred. "He kept saying how beautiful my boobs were," said the bashful Sumner. In 2004, back when this was one of London's hottest venues, receptionist Lianne Johnson claimed that she had sex with John Terry in a toilet cubicle while she had a broken leg. "There was just one thing on his mind and he wasn't going to let anything get in his way," she reported. "Not even my crutches." She added that the, er, action ended with him "giving a loud sigh like he'd scored a goal for England".

Continued p.48

John Viafara
Portsmouth

Date of birth: 27 October 1978 in Robles, Columbia.

Bought for: £900,000 from Once Caldas, July 2005.

Dumped on: Real Sociedad (loan with Southampton, undisclosed, August 2006).

Interesting detail: Jose Manuel Lopez, president of Viafara's former club Once Caldas, was put on armed guard after Columbian drug barons demanded a cut of the transfer fee.

Marks out of 10: Ability 9, Application 8, Passing 7, Tackling 7, Understanding Harry Redknapp 0.

A career in quotes

He said: "We (Colombians) have all been fans of Aston Villa for some time now because of Juan Pablo Angel. Now I will do my best to make them supporters of Portsmouth, too."

Milan Mandaric boasts: "A year ago players of this high calibre would come close to signing for us, but would end up going to other clubs. Things are different now. We're on the Premiership map."

Viafara adds: "This is my great dream and I see it being carried out. I always thought the best thing that could happen to me was to play in Europe, and if it was in England, even better, because I like the fast football, the velocity and the constant movement."

Mandaric boasts again: "He is a box-to-box midfielder – a Patrick Vieira type. This is a great signing. We're adding some real quality to our team."

Joe Jordan warns, sagely: "The language is always a big factor for a foreign player and John is struggling on that score. It is so important that we have got a teacher and interpreter fixed up for him. At the moment it is a hiccup not a problem. He looks a very good player."

Gary O'Neil adds: "It is a little bit difficult when you shout 'man on' or 'turn' or something like that and there's 20,000 people in the stadium – he can't take it in quickly."

Harry Redknapp fumes: "He doesn't speak a word of English. It is sad, it is a crazy situation. What are you supposed to do?"

George Burley signs him up: "He's good in the air and very energetic and I'm sure he will give our midfield extra balance."

George Burley adds a few days later: "He has no Championship experience. Given time he'll find the pace of the game."

THE HARD SELL

SCENE: At the wedding reception for former Manchester United and Wales full-back Clayton Blackmore, Mark Hughes seduces Craig Bellamy into signing for Blackburn, to Uefa-Cup-spot-grabbing success. The unlikely couple are divorced within a year.

Hughes: "So how do you know the groom/bride?"

Bellamy: "From the rugby club, the chapel, the male voice choir and his sheep graze my land sometimes."

Hughes: "You must be very proud. Would you care to dance?"

Bellamy: "I am not at all proud. Who told you that? And I care very much, as it happens. I did not in any way text my old partner and call him a two-left-footed clodhopper who I hoped would fall flat on his fat baldy head. I just need to find the right partner. My old partner was old and bitter. He thought the whole world revolved around him. I had to lead him everywhere. He couldn't keep up with my footwork. There was no chemistry and he always wanted to call the tune. Every time we went out I had to do the work. Whenever he wanted to eat I even had to fill up his plate for him."

Hughes: "But I've got plenty of decent partners for you. We've got a comely, stroppy, savage one who wears the daffodil with pride. Thinks Lancashire is nearer to God's own principality than Birmingham. We've got a little, fiery Celt called Dickov and Shefki, the great Finnish pine. We've even got a Norwegian one who looks like a peroxide-dipped Burmese cat. You can dance with whoever you like. Great set of lads, couldn't do enough for you. If it all kicks off, they'll back you up. If it doesn't, they'll kick it off for you."

Bellamy: "But I'm used to the biggest ballrooms in Europe. The Lyceums, the Plazas and the Palais. I don't do line dancing in the village hall. "

Hughes: "But Jack Walker built this village hall. He built this village and he left a legacy big enough to attract the best hoofers to entertain his villagers. And line dancing might just catch on"

Bellamy: "How much?"

Hughes: "All the tempered steel you'd need, the collected works of Howard Marks, all the cheese on toast you can eat and we could get Catatonia to reform to serenade your arrival."

Bellamy: "Throw in some laverbread and we'll call it a deal."

Hughes: "Deal."

Romance

THERE WAS A TIME when footballers were famous mainly for playing football. It seems ridiculous now, but it's true. These were back in the days when "private life" referred to the part of one's existence that you didn't publicise, rather than its current meaning as the part of one's existence that you don't publicise until you've got an autobiography to promote.

But even more amazingly even then, even in the days of Stanley Matthews and Nat Lofthouse, of black-and-white footage and rosettes and those wooden things that go clack-clack-clack when you spin them round, footballers wooed women. We can only guess how they did it, or even how they met them, because Chinawhite hadn't opened yet. But still they managed.

Thankfully, the world has changed since then. We now have tabloid newspapers, for a start. Where once all we knew about a footballer was whether he scored many goals, now we know details about their houses, their hobbies, how good they are in bed (Shaun Wright-Phillips: "strictly second division"; Craig Bellamy "totally blew me away") and even the size of their private parts (Claude Makelele: "huge"; Celestine Babayaro: "like a stallion"). Really, we shouldn't know any of this stuff. We shouldn't even want to know. It is a humiliation that embarrasses the nation. Even reading about it makes us feel dirty. But, hey, what are showers for? (Don't ask a footballer that question, as you're liable to get a response that involves expensive hotel suites and page 3 models.)

So famous has the concept of the footballer's wife become that they even have their own television drama. They have newspaper columns, and are invited onto reality television shows where they gleefully reveal intimate details of their husband's anatomy (Sheree Murphy found herself on *I'm a Celebrity, Get Me Out of Here* and immediately revealed that her husband Harry Kewell has "got really hairy feet and no toes", and also "the smoothest, peachiest bum ever"). Being a footballer's wife is a career, and a potentially lucrative one at that: Coleen McLouglin, with a book deal, a magazine column, a television show and a fitness video, is proof of that. Even if you don't earn anything, you could well get free access to your husband's bulging bank account, and a fortnight with the WAGs in a German spa town – and that's as good as a lottery win in anyone's (cheque)book.

So here's a handy guide to the love life of the nation's footballers. If you would like, when you grow up, to marry one, it will tell you where to hang out, what to wear, and that you should probably have plastic surgery to ensure an ample bosom. If you would like to treat your women in the way your heroes treat theirs, you will find some tips (take them to an expensive hotel room, engage in frenetic amorous activity, leave them there, and shower

Is this too much?

northern Cock

Horse-boy

other women with flirtatious text messages, would seem to be the theme). And if you are simply a voyeur (not you, Arsène), someone who takes a distasteful delight in finding out the dirty secrets of those you watch on the pitch every week, then just read and enjoy.

A footballer's wife, or FW for short, with very few exceptions, will be extremely beautiful. She might appear in glossy magazines (not that kind of magazine, sicko), or be favoured by the very finest modelling agencies. Every footballer dreams of seeing his loved one riding high in a poll of the sexiest specimens of the genre, examples of which you can regularly find in the pages of men's magazines when they can't think of a better excuse to fill their pages with pictures of semi-clad beauties. Interestingly, actually being married to a footballer is rarely among the criteria for success in such selections. In one recent example only one of the top four FWs were actually married at the time of publication. In case you're wondering, they were, in order: Cheryl Tweedy, of Girls Aloud and Ashley Cole fame, Alex Curran of Steven Gerrard fame, Sheree Murphy, who was actually married to Harry Kewell, and Wayne Rooney's fiancée Coleen McLoughlin. Much more information on each of those relationships is contained in this guide for your delectation.

Your mother probably told you that beauty was only skin deep. She may have suggested that it's what's inside that counts. When it comes to choosing a footballer's wife, this is nonsense. As the Special One's chosen one Tami Mourinho has said, as a breed they can be "obsessed with money". Sometimes they "don't know how to dress". Frequently "they have no class". Importantly, however, they normally have large breasts. It's a question of priorities.

WHAT THEY DO

Being a footballer's wife is not a hobby, it is a profession. It takes a lot of time to get right. You've got to keep up with the latest fashion trends. You've got to read every issue of *Heat* from cover to cover. You've got to spend hours in the most chichi of clothes emporia, and make sure there are photographers outside to show you've been there. You've got to spend lots of time in the gym (mainly being massaged, frequently being sprayed with fake tan, occasionally exercising). You've got to tidy the house so it's ready for when *OK!* come round to take pictures of the happy couple displaying their love for each other with the aid of so many questionable home design statements. You've got to find miraculous methods of becoming sleeker, sexier and more beautiful than ever within five minutes of giving birth. But here's a quick list of their favourite pastimes.

1. Shopping

For clothes – you can normally employ a poor person to do get the food and stuff. FWs are regularly pictured laden with bags from trendy boutiques (famously the Liverpool store Cricket, though there are others). "Sometime I hide my shopping bags in the back of my wardrobe before Steven gets home," said Alex Curran, "and when I wear something new I'll tell him I've had it for ages. I get guilt pangs about how much I've spent." It's important to look good and to keep abreast of the latest trends, for being caught in Ugg boots out of season is a hideous embarrassment. Curran and Coleen McLouglin regularly battle it out for the title of Britain's best dressed FW but Curran insists that the accolade is hers: "I think Coleen dresses really well for her age. She always looks smart but she's a bit more conservative than me. I think I'm more daring." Meeeow. Coleen, meanwhile, is trying to break into acting because, according to "a source", "she doesn't want to be seen as a footballer's wife who just goes shopping with Wayne's cash". "People don't realise there's a lot more to me than shopping," the 2005 Shopper of the Year says.

2. Have children

Families are important to footballers. Children are not just proof of their virility, they also give stars something to carry around the pitch at the end of the season instead of trophies, which they don't have because Chelsea have won them all again. Some get a little carried away – Roy Keane and his wife Theresa have five (count 'em) offspring – but most have a more sedate one or two. Children also have two further, important functions: they let a footballer prove their creativity by dreaming up silly names (Gerrard's first-born is called Lilly-Ella; Ryan Giggs went for Liberty), and they are the only acceptable way for hard-as-nails athletes to show their caring side. "I was there," said Arsenal's Lauren of the birth of his child Aliah. "I saw her come out. It was fantastic, the best experience of my life." It brings a tear to your eye. As for Gerrard, "he was there when I gave birth and he was really calm," said Curran. "He even cut the umbilical chord."

3. Have plastic surgery

Alex Curran is one of many footballers' partners to have had breast augmentation. "At school all my mates had massive boobs but I always had little ones," she says. "I always said I'd like to get bigger boobs. It's weird, but I love them." The effect of the surgery on footballers is proven by the experience of one of Wayne Bridge's former partners, who told a tabloid: "I had only just had a boob job and he was obsessed with them – stroking and kissing them. He sat for hour just gazing at them and he was asking me all about the surgery. It was as if he was transfixed ... he was fondling them for ages."

4. Domestic chores

FWs don't actually have to do these, having normally employed a poor person to do them instead, but they must talk about them in interviews to prove that they remain grounded. "I'm just a normal mum doing normal everyday things – the washing, the ironing, and making the tea," says Alex Curran. "I'm up at 7am every day. I get breakfast ready, take Lilly-Ella to nursery and stop at the shops to buy something for tea. I'm nothing like the glamorous footballer's wife stereotype." No, nothing at all. (Continued p.74)

OCTOBER

Smaller, publicity-conscious bookies begin to pay out on Chelsea winning the title ... Having introduced shadowboxing into Liverpool's training routines, Rafa Benitez comes unstuck when clumped by Darren Potter ... Arsène Wenger muses on Roman Abramovich's fortune and news that it has increased by a further £7.5 bn, "I have tried to imagine the space that much money would fill...he needs a very big room" ... Titus Bramble reveals that Graeme Souness has persuaded him to give up partying to concentrate on football. "If I go out now," he says, "it is to the cinema with Kieron Dyer" ... Before the West Brom v Blackburn match Mark Hughes admits his success as a manager has come as a surprise to his former Manchester United colleagues who had him down as "a bit of a whisperer" ... Bobby Troullis, a 15-year-old Arsenal fan, pulls out of a handshake with Djibril Cisse, sticks his thumb on his nose and waggles his fingers at the Lord of the Manor of Frodsham. His lordship clips him round the ear. "I rang 999," says the kid. "I've lost respect for him" ... Cardiff City's bonus scheme is revealed when Sam Hamann pledges that every City striker to score 20 league goals will be given a camel ... Coleen McLoughlin has her credit card rejected three times in a Madrid boutique while trying to purchase a £1,343 Chanel belt. Wayne Rooney has to be retrieved from the back of a limo to complete the transaction ... Chelsea beat Liverpool 4-1 at Anfield and immediately go into a huddle at the final whistle. "It's a team spirit kind of thing – and there were a lot of swear words," says Frank Lampard ... England players decide they don't want to watch a video of their defeat in Belfast at their latest get-together ... Joe Cole is having a sound-proofed music room built in his Esher mansion so he can strum Oasis songs without disturbing the neighbours ... Pupils at King Edward's School in Bath claim to have got hold of Gary Neville's mobile number and one reports the following exchange from the England full-back: "Shut up you fucking dick. I'm going to give your number to the police if you haven't found out who's passing my number around." When contacted by reporters Neville says: "If you make out in any way that I've been abusing kids I fucking promise you I'll take it further" ... Jose Mourinho registers his name as a trademark ... Man City win permission from Blondie to re-record Union City Blue with new lyrics as Manchester City Blue ... David Weir comes out of international retirement for Walter Smith and says embarrassed senior players used to throw sickies to get out of Berti Vogts' squads ... Vandals throw a brick through Sven's front window ... Rio Ferdinand's record label White Chalk Music is up and running and he is being advised by former Factory co-owner Tony Wilson ... Barry Ferguson blames sciatic attack on new Mercedes ... England beat Austria 1-0 and qualify for World Cup finals though Beckham is sent off. Qualification boosts the economy by £2bn according to one fatuous report ... In Cheshire, a residents group, the Edge Association in Alderley Edge, condemns its footballer residents for buying houses, demolishing them and replacing them with "highly visible buildings of breathtaking ugliness". Culprits include Rio Ferdinand, Ruud van Nistelrooy and Wayne Rooney ... Cristiano Ronaldo buys a £1.5m haunted house in Bramhall, or at least a cursed one as its three former occupants – Jaap Stam, Laurent Blanc and Kleberson – all came to grief at United ... Following qualification for the finals, Alderney announces that Messrs Beckham, Lampard, Owen and Campbell will be cast onto £25 coins ... Sven announces that he'll see the England job through to 2010 ... Paul O'Grady bans Coleen McLoughlin from appearing on his show, advising her to "get a job" ... Sepp Blatter flips, saying that new owners have infiltrated the game "throwing pornographic amounts of money" largely towards "semi-educated, sometimes foul-mouthed players demanding insane wages" ... Jose Mourinho™ spends international week at EuroDisney. "Armageddon was fantastic," he says, "water, fire, bouncing around, whee! I felt like Bruce Willis." Marcel Desailly had organised the trip, ensuring Mourinho™ enjoyed VIP treatment and didn't even have to queue ... Claudio Ranieri comes back to town to deliver his somewhat predictable verdict on Chelsea. "Fantastico!" he pronounces for the umpteenth time ... David O'Leary runs across St Andrew's after Villa's 1-0 victory there to salute Doug Ellis. He is to be charged by the FA for over-zealous and provocative celebration but he maintains that his intent was essentially benign. "He has been ill but I saw him up there all smiley-miley and I thought it would be nice to give him a wave" ... Abel Xavier claims an American over-the-counter virus treatment has caused his drugs test failure ... Victoria Beckham praises her new close friends Tom Cruise and Katie Holmes, lifelong Real Madrid fans both ... Jonathan Woodgate scores at the right end in Real's 4-1 victory over Rosenborg and leaps on the club doctor on the touchline, "A great geezer," he explains ... Victoria Beckham photographed reading Scientology book "Assists for Illnesses and Injuries" in LA ... Arsenal, 1-0 up against Manchester City, take Pires-Henry Keystone Kops penalty but still win though Pires is mortified and blames Henry ... Andy Townsend and Ally McCoist unveil their new version of the tactics truck by pontificating from a pitchside podium to much bemusement ... Nine-year-old Everton fan runs onto the pitch in their Carling Cup defeat by Middlesbrough and slide tackles Franck Queudrue ... Diego Maradona says there's nothing wrong with Wayne Rooney's temperament: "You can't be a saint and still be a success in football" ... Manchester United v Barnet ruined when Barnet goalkeeper sent off in the 3rd minute ... Prince William coaches kids at Charlton Athletic, though there are more photographers than participants ...

Managers of the month

OCTOBER

Who won the awards:

PREMIERSHIP

Paul Jewell (Wigan Athletic)
A second award on the spin for Wigan's accolade-laden manager.

CHAMPIONSHIP

Steve Coppell (Reading)
As November began Reading were still three points behind Sheffield United, despite having beaten them in October. "They now have the top spot firmly in their sights," said Chris Kamara sagely.

LEAGUE ONE

Andy Ritchie (Barnsley)
Victory in the local grudge match against Rotherham was the highlight in a month ably described by, inevitably, Chris Kamara as "tremendous".

LEAGUE TWO

Martin Ling (Leyton Orient)
Pulled the award out of the bag with wins in their last two games of the month to reach the three wins-two draws manager of the month minimum qualifying standard. "Martin deserves all the accolades," said Chris Kamara.

Who should have won the award:

Sven Goran Eriksson (England)

Perhaps the £4m annual salary makes up for his ineligibility for any major awards but having steered England to a dross-ridden home victory over Austria to secure qualification for the 2006 World Cup finals and followed that up with a vastly-improved mediocre Beckham-free win against Poland, he qualifies for a big score on the results-driven Kamara accolade-o-meter. According to one newspaper, England's qualification will boost the economy by £2 billion, a figure in no way plucked from the air, so dinging the bell on the even more prestigious Gordon Brown cash-register-o-meter.

Fired!

Still giddy after September's sackfest, league chairmen took it easy in October with not a single one of the 92 clubs ushering anybody out the door all month.

STATISTICS

Top scorers (league only):
Frank Lampard (Chelsea) – 10
Ruud Van Nistelrooy (Man Utd) – 8
Darren Bent (Charlton) – 7
Didier Drogba (Chelsea) – 6
Andy Cole (Man City) – 5

So far this season
Most assists: **Danny Murphy** (Charlton) – 6
Shots on target: **Frank Lampard** (Chelsea) – 23
Shots off target: **Mido** (Tottenham) – 16
Shots per goal: **Laurent Robert** (Portsmouth) – 32
Most fouls: **Kevin Davies** (Bolton) – 35
Most fouled: **Luis Boa Morte** (Fulham) – 38

Match of the month
MIDDLESBROUGH 4
MANCHESTER UTD 1

In which we discovered: 1) If Manchester United can make Middlesbrough look like Brazil circa 1970, they really are in trouble; 2) Rio Ferdinand's ability to concentrate is on a par with that of a recently divorced middle-aged man in charge of the remote control on an unexpected Sunday night in with golf and football to choose from who has just discovered a raunchy Girls Aloud special on MTV; 3) Boro's next home match draws 12,900 fans to a Uefa Cup tie, a drop in five days of 17,600, the biggest percentage seasonal fluctuation in the Premiership, making the smug away fans' chant "You're only here to see United/ Arsenal/ Chelsea" seem more appropriate than usual; 4) A midfield of Fletcher, Smith, Scholes and Park requires only the transfer window purchase of matchstick cats and dogs to make up the cast of Brian and Michael's Mancunian magnum opus; 5) That results like this are never blessings in disguise, unless inviting Roy Keane into the MUTV studio to deconstruct his team so viciously that the programme can never be shown and the midfielder is swiftly ousted constitutes a "blessing". Three days later United lose in Paris against Lille.

Top of the table

	P	W	D	L	F	A	GD	Pts
1 CHELSEA	11	10	1	0	28	6	22	31
2 WIGAN ATHLETIC	10	7	1	2	11	5	6	22
3 TOTTENHAM	11	5	5	1	13	7	6	20
4 MANCHESTER CITY	11	6	2	3	14	9	5	20
5 BOLTON WANDERERS	11	6	2	3	13	11	2	20

Bottom of the table

	P	W	D	L	F	A	GD	Pts
16 ASTON VILLA	11	2	3	6	10	19	-9	9
17 WEST BROM	11	2	2	7	9	21	-12	8
18 EVERTON	10	2	1	7	3	12	-9	7
19 BIRMINGHAM CITY	11	1	3	7	7	16	-9	6
20 SUNDERLAND	11	1	2	8	10	21	-11	5

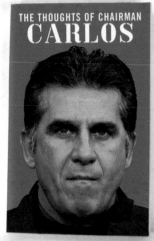
THE THOUGHTS OF CHAIRMAN
CARLOS

CARLOS QUEIROZ'S
FOOTBALL HANDBOOK
MODULE 3 – PERFECTING THE 4–5–1

" **RESEARCH SHOWS THAT** my favourite system is also the best system. It is so easily adaptable, giving the coach and the intelligent player a structure around which to control a football match. With just a signal from the touchline the defensive midfield player drops back between the centre-halves to make it 5-4-1 or, if the team needs extra defensive steel (and let's face it which teams don't?) another defensive midfielder can supplement the centre back positions to make it 6-3-1. Ah, you say, does this not leave the midfield understrength? Not if the adjustment is also made at the top of the formation, and the "1" retreats to compensate, making it 6-4-0. Then, when counter-attacking, the auxiliary fourth centre-half, or, perhaps more accurately, temporary centre-quarter, quickly rejoins the midfield group to make it 5-5-0, two banks of five, a revolutionary new approach to security. This works best with dynamic, versatile young men with minds so open tactical implants can easily be inserted. These quiet and polite young players would never be so impertinent to suggest such sophisticated stratagems would be better served by being thrust "up" one's "bollocks". Here my ideal team template captures the transition from 4-5-1 to 5-4-1: "

Van der Sar

O'Shea   O'Shea   O'Shea   O'Shea   O'Shea

O'Shea   O'Shea   O'Shea   O'Shea

O'Shea

Theo's Diary

1 2 3 4 5 6 7 8 9 10 11 12 13 14 me!

I scored three goals in three games this month which was a lot of fun because I hadn't scored even once since I started playing with the big men and I'm used to scoring all the time normally. It's different when you score with the big men because afterwards these people with microphones ask you lots of questions. They call it an interview but that's wrong because I had an interview when I started school and all I had to do was some colouring in.

Gordon Strachan's cheeseboard
Stilton

THIS VENERABLE BRITISH CHEESE proves that there's no substitute for age and experience. Old, unsightly and salty it might be but you can usually get away with such things north of the border. Liberally sprinkle your cheeseboard with lumps of the gnarled classic and, though the stench of decay may be ripe and it would be thrown away in other cultures, you can still win plaudits in Scotland for astute husbandry. After a year or so the most mature Stiltons start to go off. Ensure you either replace it with a steady supply of cheap, veteran curds that others have discarded or retire to England and take the cheeseboard off the menu for good before you get found out.

Welcome to... Wigan

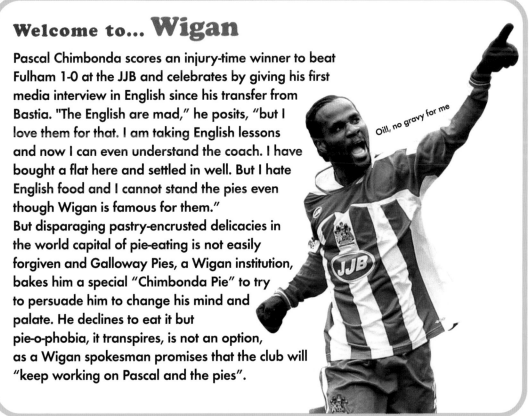

Oill, no gravy for me

Pascal Chimbonda scores an injury-time winner to beat Fulham 1-0 at the JJB and celebrates by giving his first media interview in English since his transfer from Bastia. "The English are mad," he posits, "but I love them for that. I am taking English lessons and now I can even understand the coach. I have bought a flat here and settled in well. But I hate English food and I cannot stand the pies even though Wigan is famous for them."

But disparaging pastry-encrusted delicacies in the world capital of pie-eating is not easily forgiven and Galloway Pies, a Wigan institution, bakes him a special "Chimbonda Pie" to try to persuade him to change his mind and palate. He declines to eat it but pie-o-phobia, it transpires, is not an option, as a Wigan spokesman promises that the club will "keep working on Pascal and the pies".

SVEN GORAN ERIKSSON'S Dossier

+ + + + + + OCTOBER 2005 + + + + + + +

Psst... psst, Sven... over here

I was loading the dishwasher the other day while Nancy was waiting for me in the bedroom and I thought to myself, because it is here that I do a lot of my thinking, if I am to win the World Cup maybe I will have to change, and if I am to win the respect of this nation I must change too. I must be more hard of head, in my dealings with the fairer sex, in the world of business and also with the footballers. No longer shall the tabloid newspapers be able to say I have had relations with inappropriate women. Instead they will be remarking with admiration on my business dealings with the most powerful sultans and sheikhs, and noting with considerable reverence my new-found ability to drop any underperforming players, except Owen Hargreaves, and replace them with the nation's finest young talents.

In this way England will keep appreciating me, and they will continue to offer me ludicrous contracts until I am ready to leave and seek a new challenge somewhere in continental Europe. I was leaving a football ground 10 minutes before the end of the game the other day and I thought to myself, because it is at moments like these that I consider matters of football with the greatest clarity, maybe I am going wrong here. Maybe my compulsion to watch as much Premiership football as physically possible is barking me up the wrong tree, it is pandering to the wills of other managers, weaker managers, people born sucking a silver spoon, who in order to take their position near the top of the management tree have had to fight their way from somewhere like Essex while I have strained and stumbled across the icy tundras of snow-capped Sweden sweating through every pore, and I have attacked the treacherous slopes of Mount Soccer with second-hand crampons – but still I have reached its summit.

So the other day, while I was in the toilet between courses during dinner in an exclusive restaurant with the chairman of a big club who might one day be in a position to offer me a ludicrous contract, I made a decision, because it is at such times that I make a lot of my decisions. I decided that I would no longer be dictated to by the managers in the Premierboat, because I may be a quiet man from Torsby but my opinion is important and my decisions make a lot of noise. And I will not be forced into anything by fans who watch only their team and care only for their own interests. I will pick someone new, someone fresh. I will find a talent they have never seen. And if I have never seen him either, so much the better. I will show the world that me, predictable Sven, the Swede called Svennis with the pointy features and the designer glasses, can surprise everyone. Including myself. And with that decision made, I can get on with keeping true to the rest of my new resolutions. Now, I was recently contacted by a very wealthy and powerful sheikh. Where did I put his number?

Not now, go away.
I'm thinking about tits and money...

Josemi
Liverpool

Date of birth: 15 November 1979 in Torremolinos, Spain
Otherwise known as: Jose Miguel Gonzales Rey
Nickname: Doh Rey Mi – because he's got so fa to go
Family business: A hairdressers in Torremolinos
Bought for: £2m from Malaga, July 2004
Sold for: Not so much sold as swapped for Villarreal's Jan Kromkamp, January 2006.
Likes: Spain, Spanish sun
Dislikes: England, English rain
Vital statistics: Liverpool 2004/05: League games started 13;
Fouls committed 25; Yellow cards 6; Red cards 1

Liverpool 2005/06: League games started 3;
Fouls committed 4; Yellow cards 1; Red cards 0

Villarreal 2005/06: League games started 5;
Fouls committed 16; Yellow cards 3; Red cards 0

Marks out of 10: Desire 7; ability 3; defending 4; linguistic skills 1

A career in quotes

On arrival: "I will work to make sure things turn out well. It's an offer I couldn't refuse. It's a proud moment for everybody connected with me. I'm really happy."

Rafael Benitez adds: "I know this player and he is good in defence, good in the air and can make this team stronger."

Two weeks later: "My mum and sister have a men's hairdressers in Torremolinos. When I was with Malaga, all the other players had their hair cut free of charge – and nobody complained."

After the first season: "It took me a while to adapt to the pace and the physical side of the game here but I will be a lot better this season"

Benitez adds: "It is difficult to play in another country. Josemi has tried to learn English and he's improved a lot but for him and his family it has been hard."

A year in: "At the moment it is almost going too well I would say. My wife is also very happy. I feel very at home in the city and comfortable within the team."

A few weeks later, Benitez adds: "Josemi is a very good professional but he needs to go to Spain to see the sun every day because he's from Malaga. That is the reason why so many British people go there on holiday."

When he left: "My family and I suffered a lot. I was not a happy person. It was difficult to open the door to my home and see my family so unhappy, too. Every person is a different kind of animal and some people can adjust quicker and better living abroad."

THE HARD SELL

S C E N E : The players' car park at Arsenal's training ground

Henry: Psst, Robert! Venez vite!

Pires: What is it, Thierry? And please stop talking in French – the person making up this conversation doesn't speak it very well.

Henry: Sorry, mon ami. It's just that I've got something for you. One of those DVDs you like so much. You know, the ones that offer the special finish.

Pires: Mmmm, there's nothing like that moment of satisfaction. The ultimate high.

Henry: Well, you've not seen anything yet. This is better than everything you've seen before.

Pires: Even that Swedish stuff that Freddie gave me?

Henry: Believe me. This is Dutch. They're the best. They're the most daring. There is nothing they wouldn't do. This has got it all – three-on-ones, people taking up some amazing positions, and you should see the tricks! Once you've seen this you'll be dreaming about it for weeks.

Pires: And can we act out some of the best scenes ourselves like we did with the other ones?

Henry: But of course. I tell you, this will really blow your mind.

Pires: Enough! I want it. What's it called?

Henry: It's called: "Johann Cruyff: His Greatest Goals and Games"

Pires: Cruyff? You're right, it is going to be better than Freddie's Henrik Larsson compilation.

Henry: And I know exactly which bit we're going to act out on the pitch. There's this penalty he did, it's on the DVD. It's unbelievable. He doesn't even shoot – he just taps the ball to his team-mate who knocks the ball back across goal for Cruyff to tap in.

Pires: That sounds amazing. We'll do it.

Two weeks later...

Henry: I can't believe it! It looked so easy on TV.

Pires: Bloody DVDs, you can't trust them. It's all special effects these days.

Henry: Not to worry. I've found a new one that we'll definitely be able to manage.

Pires: What's it called?

Henry: Peter Crouch's ultimate ball-juggling.

The Lord of the Manor of Frodsham coat of arms

WHEN THE LIVERPOOL STRIKER Djibril Cisse bought the £2m Ridge Manor estate in the leafy Cheshire town of Frodsham, he also inherited a title which dates back to the Domesday Book. It's unlikely that the Cisse family have their own coat of arms, so we thought we'd knock one up for him...

1. Two parrots

A rare African grey parrot ordered by Cisse was one of two birds stolen from Line Star Tropicals in Tarvin last year after thieves chiselled a hole in the shop's wall from the vacant premises next door and swiped the pair. The other was the shop's own pet parrot, Golly Grey.

2. A fox

Cisse banned the Cheshire Forest Hunt from using his nine acres after a written appeal from the League Against Cruel Sports. "He has set a fantastic example and we would ask all landowners to follow his lead," they said.

3. Six cars

Ridge Manor House has six bedrooms, four bathrooms, three stables, a ballroom, a tennis court, an indoor pool, a chauffeur's cottage and garage space for six (count 'em) cars.

4. A castle

Sadly not Frodsham Castle, destroyed back in 1654 after a catastrophic fire, but Bodelwyddan Castle in Denbighshire, North Wales, where Cisse married the hairdressing consultant Jude Littler, a single mother seven years his senior, last summer. Superstars in attendance included France team-mates Zinedine Zidane and Thierry Henry and Shaun Wright-Phillips. "He does not act like a superstar at all," said Lillian Littler, his grandmother-in-law. "He's a lovely, lovely man. I should imagine she fell for his charm."

5. A head with something silly on it, like a pineapple or a rabbit

If you're going to marry a hairdressing consultant, you should end up with something relatively fashionable on your head. Instead, Cisse prefers to model a regularly-changing line-up of absurdities. He has not, as yet, walked out wearing a rabbit but it's only a matter of time.

6. Some very trendy clothes

Cisse has his very own fashion label, Klubb 9. "I always wanted to stand out from my mates by having my own style," he says. Well, he certainly does that.

7. A needle

Cisse doesn't confine his elaborate artworks to the top of his head. Thanks to his tattooist friends there's one on the side of his head, not to mention his back and legs. Having picked up the habit in France, he's found a home from home at Liverpool's Tribalife studio.

8. A boxing glove

His lordship sometimes finds it hard to control his temper. In 2005 he was cautioned for hitting a 15-year-old boy in London while filming an advert. In January 2006 it was reported that he had assaulted his pregnant wife but the villain turned out to be someone else in the town (and the victim someone else's wife, presumably).

9. A barely noticeable shade of red

That's Cisse blushing after appearing naked on a French calendar this year.

Nightclubs

Continued from p.29

BOUJIS, LONDON

43 Thurloe Street, SW7 2LQ
Tel. 020 7584 2000 / www.boujus.com

A boutique nightclub, which is a polite way of saying it's small. Still, it manages to make a virtue out of it and boasts of a string of successes in the latest London Club & Bar Awards. It's not just for footballers - properly famous people go here, including Christina Aguilera and our future king, Prince William.

Tabloid tales

Another Chelsea haunt, Wayne Bridge and Eidur Gudjohnsen have been seen here, while this is where Frank Lampard headed to celebrate England's 3-2 friendly win over Argentina last November. The Ashes victory party ended here, when Ashley Giles, Kevin Pietersen and Michael Vaughan were the last men standing a full 30 hours after the festivities began.

KENSINGTON ROOF GARDENS, LONDON

99 Kensington High Street, W8 5SA
Tel. 020 7937 7994 / www.roofgardens.com

Flamingo-motifed London rooftop venue, not really known for attracting footballers but worth including for a single noteworthy incident.

Tabloid tales

Paris Hilton was reported to have "hit on" Frank Lampard at the Warner Records Brits after-show party in February 2006. He snubbed her advances, though she then followed him to the EMI bash at the Baglioni hotel.

FUNKY BUDDHA, LONDON

15 Berkeley Street, Mayfair W1J 8DY
Tel. 020 7495 2596 / www.fblondon.co.uk

"The epitome of all that today's affluent London club-goer requires", they boast. "A unique and innovative destination venue". That's them again. Expect a high-end, vaguely oriental theme. And cocktail sausages, which make an unexpected appearance on the canapé menu.

Tabloid tales

The greatest event in the history of the club came in May 2005, when "four jealous models" fought with each other for the right to accompany Celestine Babayaro and Peter Crouch away from the club. "I'm not surprised they were fighting over him," said one of the former's conquests. "Celestine is like a stallion and can satisfy any woman completely." The fight was apparently sparked by one girl, screaming that "I was talking to them first, you effing bitch". But that is just one highlight. Others include Anton Ferdinand and David Beckham's little sister Joanne with "their hands all over each other", according to an "eyewitness". Less successful was Eric Cantona, who tried to chat up a Daily Mirror reporter. He allegedly asked her, and her female chums, if they "kiss each other or have sex sometimes", and invited them to his house "for some girl-on-girl action". Fulham's Zat Knight was spotted "eyeing up the ladies" in January. Page 3 model Lauren Pope, former flame of Prince Harry and, er, Peter Crouch, attracted Jermaine Jenas to her 22nd birthday party here. Ashley Cole subverted the stereotype by coming on a night out and ignoring all the women. "He just wasn't interested," a "spy" said. Dwight Yorke (inevitably) had a bad experience here when someone grabbed his £37,000 Franck Muller Conquistador King watch. He got it back, though, and the thief got three and a half years.

Continued p.77

ON THE ANALYST'S COUCH WITH
TONY ADAMS

Sol Campbell: "Tone, can you help me? I've forgotten how to defend."

Big Tone: "The courage you have demonstrated in admitting you have a problem is more than the courage you will require to make a breakthrough. Your loss of form is a mark of low self esteem, your loss of pace a paradigm of your blocked psyche. Your cognitive tool is wounded, defeat has become a co-dependent on your resources, it needs amendingment. A couple of days intensitivity with me and we can unblock. I am the Mr Muscle of the damaged pipes of your soul. We are all crying out for actualisation. Take a step forward, three to the side, then shine a torch underneath your predicament. If you can envision your solution in a very real holistic sense then closure can be surmounted and first your head and then the ball will become round again."

Sol Campbell: "Sorry? I don't understand."

Big Tone: "Perhaps my colleague Professor Willie Young can help."

Willie Young: "What's the problem?"

Sol Campbell: "I've become hesitant."

Willie Young: "Simple. Stop arsing about and thwack the bleedin' knacker into touch pronto."

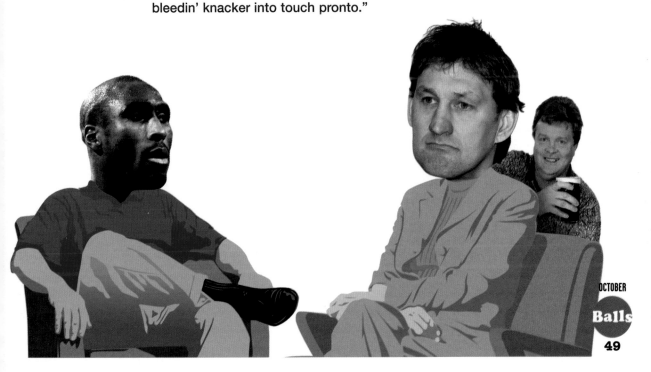

NOVEMBER

Having played the pundit and had the plug pulled, Roy Keane's condemnation of his team-mates performance when getting tonked at Middlesbrough is leaked. "There is talk about putting this right in January and bringing new players in. We should be doing the opposite – we should be getting rid of people in January," he says. Or November as it transpires ... Hearts chairman George Foulkes resigns nine days after George Burley's resignation accusing owner Vladimir Romanov of "ruthlessness" and "acting like a megalomaniac". He should know, he used to work for Clare Short ... Portsmouth's Laurent Robert is fined £50,000 for refusing to be a substitute at Sunderland. Something funny seems to come over him in the north-east of England ... Jermaine Pennant is fined two weeks' wages for turning up to training drunk and Steve Bruce issues another "final, final warning" ... Neil Warnock reveals he relieves his stress by keeping fish and has named two of his prized specimens after the two people he hates most in football – Stan Ternent and Gary Megson ... Stan Collymore is detained by the Australian police after a fracas outside a nightclub ... Referees' boss Keith Hackett is accused of covering up the punishment of Graham Poll. The Tring official was banned for two games after climbing over cars during a bender on a fitness course in July. At least it showed the fitness sessions were working ... Frank Lampard is currently serving an indefinite ban, at least from dressing his daughter Luna after his partner Elen, a staunch Barcelona fan, came home to find the baby dressed in a Chelsea kit and said "she's not going out in that" ... A 20-year-old Norwegian Start and Manchester Utd fan is arrested for burning down a Kristiansand police station after both clubs lost in weekend fixtures ... Jose Mourinho accuses Arsène Wenger of being a voyeur. "There are some guys who, when they are at home, have a big telescope to see what happens in other families. He speaks, speaks, speaks about Chelsea," quips, quips, quips the Portuguese manager ... Coleen McLoughlin has turned her mind to the burgeoning H5N1 panic: "Bird flu is scary. I had flu recently and was miserable. I'll certainly stay away from chickens for a while." Not the first time her household will impose a ban on old birds ... Preston's Billy Davies offers a cut-price remedy to cure David Nugent's lethargy: "He's worn out but we won't be sending him on holiday. He can have 100 sunbed sessions next week instead". Davies is quickly offered employment by Dale Winton

... Freddy Shepherd insists that much injured striker Kieron Dyer "has lived like a monk" in an effort to get fit. Prayer? Flagellation? Mead making? ... Omanayi Alabi, an illegal immigrant, is arrested for claiming over £1m in benefits in the names of David Seaman, Ashley Cole, Raymond Parlour and other Arsenal players ... While his P45 is being prepared, Roy Keane watches United beat Chelsea with a goal from Darren "I can't understand why people in Scotland rave about him. He is wandering around as if he is lost" Fletcher ... Sir Alex, asked whether the Keane criticism and stuttering Champions League form is the most pressure he's faced, offers us a rare glimpse into the modern media savvy skills of elite management. No, he says, "it's all bollocks" ... Gary Lineker takes a break from lounging about in a shirt with one too many buttons undone to sign up to be the voice of Underground Ernie in the eponymous CBBC animated series. He will play a grey tube train, but in fear of being typecast, wants this one to eat electricity rather than crisps . . ."I can reassure the fans and players I will not be walking away, " says Gazza after another Kettering defeat ... Charlton skipper Luke Young sends a club official on a £400 taxi errand after forgetting to pack his boots for the away trip to Blackburn. They lose 4-1 even with the magic boots ... Laurent Robert pays his fine but asks his colleagues, "why don't you pass the ball to me?" Perhaps because you refuse to play? ... Rio Ferdinand claims that United's win over Chelsea was "one for the gaffer". The fact that Chelsea currently manage around 30 a season for their gaffer escapes him ... "Wembley may not be ready for the Cup final," Brian Barwick admits. But which year is he talking about? 2009? ... Winston "£693,000 earned per game played" Bogarde officially retires five years after his last league appearance ... "I believe we're as good as Arsenal and Man Utd," claims Newcastle's Scott Parker who is supposed to have a strained hamstring, not a strained brain ... England's players will earn £300k each if they win the World Cup ... Bryan Robson tells his West Brom players they need to get more angry with each other. Kanu makes a start by refusing to say "you're welcome" when Geoff Horsfield thanks him for complimenting his eau de toilette ... David Beckham is spotted buying lingerie at Agent Provocateur in Manchester ... Hajduk Split defender Goran Granic says they're losing matches because he must "avoid committing fouls" now he's become a Catholic ... Millwall's midfielder David Livermore thinks lack of team spirit if the cause of their poor run and that a massive booze up is what's needed ... David Seaman finally has his ponytail chopped off on TV show *This Morning* to raise money for charity ... "Instinct", the David Beckham aftershave, goes on sale. It has the intoxicating aroma of money ... Brazilian World Cup winner Dunga buys a £1 m stake in QPR ... John Terry caught romping with 30D blonde Jenny Barker in his Bentley ... England players enjoy a "bonding session" with Johnny Vegas ... England shrug off Argentinian taunts that they're "poofs" and "whores" and beat Argentina 3-2. ... Man City defender Sun Jihai travels to Dalian in China to have a haircut. Beat that Ivan Campo ... Mike Tyson offers Wayne Rooney some careers guidance: "he can't be a mature adult, a scholar and all dignified at this stage of life." Well indeed, or at any other stage either ...

Managers of the month

NOVEMBER

Who won the awards:

PREMIERSHIP

Rafael Benitez (Liverpool)
Still no debut goal for Peter Crouch but two each for Djibril Cisse, Fernando Morientes and Luis Garcia in four wins with four clean sheets in the month.

CHAMPIONSHIP

Steve Coppell (Reading)
In a commendably accolade-free month, Chris Kamara's panel give the silver Coca-Cola bottle to Steve Coppell, recognised for Reading's unbeaten run since losing their opening fixture of the season. "Steve is slowly moulding the team into what he wants," says Kamara. "Slowly"? Miaow.

LEAGUE ONE

Dave Penney (Doncaster Rovers)
Would have got the neutrals' award for the look on David O'Leary's face when Rovers knocked Villa out of the Carling Cup this month but the award, Kamara sternly reminds us, is for league form alone and the South Yorkshire side were unbeaten in three.

LEAGUE TWO

John Ward (Cheltenham)
Judge-pleasing, eye-catching turnaround for the Robins who bounced back from losing four of five in October to win, in the panel's words, three on the spin. "John Ward has done a brilliant job," opines Kamara.

Who should have won the award:

Sir Alex Ferguson (Manchester United)
Okay, United lost to Middlesbrough in their last fixture in October as the fine suit of 4-5-1 he had been persuaded to wear for the occasion by his assistant actually revealed him to be stark bollock naked. And yes, United promptly lost to Lille in their next match, essentially knocking themselves out of the Champions' League at the group stage barely four months after a £790 million takeover. Between the two matches, however, Fergie's captain Roy Keane with a career-terminating assessment of his team-mates. The midfielder's advice provoked the return of the Ferginator, an empurpled one-man hornet's nest and in first upbraiding then sacking his favoured son, he regained control of the club and beat Chelsea to kick-start a five-match unbeaten run.

Fired!

Neale Cooper (Gillingham)
Alain Perrin (Portsmouth)
Colin Hendry (Blackpool)

STATISTICS

Top scorers (league only):

Frank Lampard (Chelsea) – 11
Ruud Van Nistelrooy (Man Utd) – 10
Thierry Henry (Arsenal) – 8
Aiyegbeni Yakubu (Middlesboro) – 8

So far this season
Most shots on target:
Frank Lampard (Chelsea) – 27
Most shots per goal:
Laurent Robert (Portsmouth) – 34

Most shots without scoring:
Fabio Rochemback (Middlesboro) – 34
Most offsides: **Darren Bent**
(Charlton) – 20
Most fouls without being booked:
Andy Gray (Sunderland) – 27
Most shots on target: **Chelsea** – 113
Most shots off target: **Chelsea** – 99
Most corners: **Everton** – 84
Most woodwork strikes: **Aston Villa** – 5

Match of the month
WIGAN 1 NEWCASTLE 0

In which we discovered: 1) That resting nine regular players proves no hindrance to newly-promoted sides when taking on Newcastle United. 2) That just because the oft-repeated phrase, "Shay Given really doesn't deserve this" is a cliché doesn't make it any less true. 3) That Newcastle United fans below the age of 10 might confidently assume that their manager's name is "Graeme Sounessout". 4) That someone could have slipped something into Sounessout's tea last January when he spent £12 million on Celestine Babayaro, Amdy Faye and Jean-Alain Boumsong in an eight-day splurge. 5) That an enraged Freddy Shepherd looks remarkably like a King Edward potato. 6) If Wigan's reserves are this good, they're easily staying up. 7) If Paul Jewell wants an A-list job, the David Brent beige bomber will have to go.

		P	W	D	L	F	A	GD	Pts
Top of the table									
1	**CHELSEA**	14	12	1	1	33	7	26	37
2	**MANCHESTER UNITED**	13	8	3	2	21	13	8	27
3	**ARSENAL**	13	8	2	3	22	10	12	26
4	**LIVERPOOL**	13	7	4	2	15	8	7	25
5	**WIGAN ATHLETIC**	13	8	1	4	16	10	6	25
Bottom of the table									
16	**EVERTON**	13	4	1	8	5	16	-11	13
17	**WEST BROM**	14	3	3	8	15	24	-9	12
18	**PORTSMOUTH**	14	2	4	8	11	20	-9	10
19	**BIRMINGHAM CITY**	13	2	3	8	8	17	-9	9
20	**SUNDERLAND**	15	1	2	12	12	30	-18	5

CARLOS QUEIROZ'S
FOOTBALL HANDBOOK
MODULE 4

THE THOUGHTS OF CHAIRMAN CARLOS

" **AND SO THE** curtains close on a great career as Roy Keane takes his leave of Old Trafford. When I came here to mentor him he was a rampaging, all-action, British-type midfielder – a crowd-pleaser. You are such philistines, you love all that conspicuous effort, goal-scoring and the like. Anyone can do that. But I got hold of Roy and said, "Do you want to be remembered as a swanky comic book hero or as one of the all-time greats like Wilkins, Dunga and Deschamps?" And so began the great transformation as Roy became the anchor man, rarely leaving a five-metre square box in front of the back four and hardly ever succumbing to a whim to cross the halfway line. And look what we won with him playing in this way. We won the league in 2003 and the Cup in 2004, two trophies in four years can't be bad for a club as prestigious as this. And I was his role model, I know that for sure, because as he was leaving he shouted across to me something about me being a "Portuguese anchor" and I was touched. "

'anker

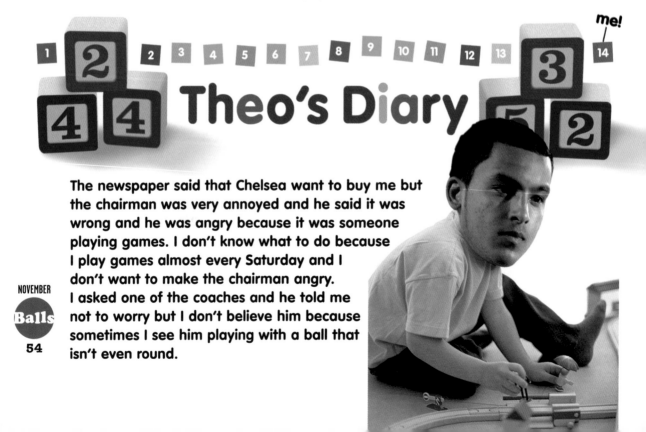

me!

1 2 2 3 4 5 6 7 8 9 10 11 12 13 3 14

4 4 # Theo's Diary 5 2

The newspaper said that Chelsea want to buy me but the chairman was very annoyed and he said it was wrong and he was angry because it was someone playing games. I don't know what to do because I play games almost every Saturday and I don't want to make the chairman angry. I asked one of the coaches and he told me not to worry but I don't believe him because sometimes I see him playing with a ball that isn't even round.

Rafa Benitez's cheeseboard
Manchego & Lancashire

I DON'T STICK with one type of cheese like some Scots fromage fanciers I could mention. No, I like a combination of Spanish and local produce. Yes, both share some characteristics. They are intense but have a propensity for crumbliness. The Lancashire element is cheap and more robust and compliments a great toast, or five, and has won numerous continental awards despite a lack of sophistication. The Manchego, on the other hand, is expensive and takes longer to settle but with careful nurturing can be a very strong companion even if it has a very poor finish. They usually work well together but if you get the quantities wrong they can leave a foul taste in your mouth.

Welcome to...
Doncaster

Young Scottish striker Ross McCormack hopes to have a big future ahead of him at Rangers, having proved himself last season during an occasionally testing loan spell south of the border. "Doncaster is a little town and the scenery wasn't great but I enjoyed the football," he said after scoring five goals in 12 starts for Rovers. Undistracted as he was by the need for sightseeing, he also had time to perform some unfamiliar chores. "Down in Doncaster I had to do everything for myself," he said. "I had to take home my kit and wash it and dry it."

FOOTBALLERS' HOUSES

Here's what the team at *Balls!* have learnt:

1. THE ARBITERS OF TASTE

Footballers are as likely to buy a house in the normal way – trawl the estate agents, get telephone calls every day for two months promising "the ideal home for you but it's 50% more than you can afford to spend but there's room for movement, you really must see it, what do you mean we showed it to you last week?" – as they are to buy a suit from Mr Byrite. Made-to-measure homes take all the hassle away, all they've got to do is turn up once, look at the plans, tell them whether they want 14 or 15 integrated televisions and sign a cheque, usually with six noughts. Fact (or at least a statistic made up by someone else): footballers spend £85 million a year on property.

The design gurus most likely to get the commission are Mayad Allos for players in the south and Dawn Ward for those up north, property developers of such efficiency and elegance that they would be guaranteed to get Sarah Beeney purring like a cat stuck in a kipper box.

Allos, reports the *Daily Telegraph* in a breathless profile on its property pages, is a 40-year-old Iraq-born businessman who has erected a string of Xanadus in formerly sleepy Surrey villages. He has built the homes currently occupied by Jamie Redknapp, Graeme Le Saux and Ian Walker and if he could put the equivalent of a royal warrant marque outside his office, it would feature the Chelsea lion as he is the developer by appointment to Jose Mourinho's squad. His houses range from £2 million-£6.5 million and some feature indoor swimming pools that can be transformed into discos, "42in plasma screen televisions in each room [and] a canopy of twinkling diodes that simulate the stars at night."

Ward is the wife of Ashley Ward, a forward whose transfer to your club usually meant that relegation was imminent. She oversaw the construction of Wayne Rooney's £3.5 million home in Prestbury, built on the plot where the 1930s villa they had originally bought stood before they demolished it. Their new home is a three-storey, six-bedroom affair with the obligatory swimming pool, Jacuzzi, cinema and pillared entrance. Her company, Bilton Ward, has recently redeveloped a farm in Wilmslow and put up four properties that she says she "could have sold to footballers but I haven't because I wanted them to be on show for a short time."

Giving the *Manchester Evening News* its annual tour of her kitchen, Ward points out her signature features: "They are always big enough for dining and living. I always insist on the top appliances – Subzero, Wolfe, Viking and Aga. My central island has a built-in wine cooler by Subzero and our other appliances include an Amana American style fridge/freezer and a Viking Professional gas range. I always use 60mm New York edge granite which is three times the thickness of the standard." They get to go upstairs too, to see how Ashley enjoys the luxury normally experienced by one of Michael Winner's "princesses" on a weekend break. "I always design my houses with a big master suite," Ward says, "featuring a lounge, dressing room and bathroom as standard." But do they come with own "tea and coffee making facilities", complimentary shortbread and £9 nuts chilled in a beige fridge?

Another Wilmslow resident, Laura McCree, fittingly enough a "star" of BBC's *Changing Rooms*, is also helping Coleen McLoughlin to titivate Wayne's pile. "I'm one of the biggest designers for Premiership footballers at the moment," she reveals, "because a lot of my best friends are footballers and they have supported me from the early days of my career. It's like a family and it's all recommendations." And that shows just how much the game has changed. Where Paul Gascoigne had Jimmy "Five Bellies" Gardner, a stranger one confidently predicts to *Elle Decoration*, now the new breed of wallpaper-savvy footballers, like nothing better than to pal up with friends of Lawrence Llewellyn Bowen to discuss pantone palettes.

2. TRUE COLOURS

Premiership teams play in a variety of colours: scarlet, vermillion, raspberry, royal blue, primrose and humbug stripes but at home Premiership players choose from a limited colour chart. Basically their homes are decorated in minimalist Toblerone hues, a variety of whites and browns, suggesting purity, discretion, classicism and a lack of imagination. The whites tend not to be of the Daz doorstep challenge variety but are richer, ranging across the albino spectrum from "Captain Bird's Eye's beard" to "pipe-smoker's dentures". The ubiquitous flowers and never-to-be-lit candles all fit the same narrow scheme – what used to be called off-white but is now known as "crème brulée" or even "white chocolate". In the few rooms without exposed floorboards the carpets too are ivory, necessitating the removal of shoes to preserve the virginal look. The inspiration seems to be John and Yoko loping around an Ascot grange the size of Waterloo station whilst imagining no possessions. That ethereal look is not difficult to replicate. Indeed it's easy if you try, as Robbie Savage proudly demonstrated on MTV when showing off his wintry interiors and allowing the cameras to see the centrepiece of his bedroom, a white leather bed of such proportions it gave his sleeping quarters the exclusive air of mid-January Murmansk.

3. ALL MOD CONS

The ultimate in controlling your entire house from a device that would not have been out of place on Captain Kirk's console chair is offered by a company called Lifestyle Scene. And who better to run such a company than three men intimately acquainted with success on the football field? That's right, Jody Morris, Andy Myers and Andrew Impey. Well, at least they know a few men who have been successful on the football field.

Their business, Impey explains, was thought up during Morris' wedding, a commendably innovative approach from the groom, a role which usually consists of rictus-grinning and mouthing platitudes to people they've not seen for 20 years and are unlikely to ever meet again. "The three of us were pretty well pissed," Impey admits, "but it still seemed a good idea the next morning." John Terry is one of their first clients and will benefit, like the singer Craig David who has extolled the virtues of such labour-saving technology that banishes forever the toil of standing up to turn on a lamp, from "home automation, luxury push-button systems that control everything from lighting, curtains, TV, security, the lot."

Sheree Murphy, aka Mrs Harry Kewell, has not yet been Lifestyle Scened but let MTV see that integrated electronics were not the be all and end all of celebrity living. Not content with a television in each room, she has had two installed in her bathroom, at either ends of the tub so that its occupants need never adopt the seating arrangements of Redgrave and Pinsent to keep their eyes glued to episodes of Date My Mom. Walk-in wardrobes naturally feature prominently in her Cheshire Southfork as well as designated handbag and shoe cupboards to showcase her hobbies.

4. SHE SELLS SANCTUARIES

Even though they're usually engaged in their profession six days a week, if only the mornings mostly, footballers still need a place in which they can hide from their partners. For normal folk this is usually a box room pompously dubbed an office where computer games can surreptitiously be played without provoking a furious row or, failing that, a pub. But footballers are too rich to slope off to a cubby hole or wooden hut and, believing themselves trapped indoors by hordes of autograph seekers, won't go near a pub. So they bring the pub home, or, more accurately, having misspent their youths training and playing matches, they interpret their quaint, antiquated perceptions of what an ideal pub is like in the shape of the "games room". They stop short of a designated dominoes arena, but those other stalwarts from traditional hostelries are all in place.

There, amid the unopened man of the match champers bottles, they can relax as Joanna Taylor, wife of Tottenham's Danny Murphy, explains: "He has all the things any man could want – a dart board, a pool table, Sky TV and a fridge. It is also the place where he has his trophies and memorabilia ... I go in to clean and that's about it." Ever the grandee, Sir Alex Ferguson has a snooker table in his, Steven Gerrard has the glass doors of his retreat etched with scenes from Istanbul 2005 and Wayne Rooney has his 20th birthday present, a £3,300 jukebox, because multiple CD changers and £10,000 worth of stereo equipment can't quite cut the audio mustard.

5. A CAUTIONARY TALE

But lest one think that all players aspire to the Grand Designs prescribed lifestyle of pristine 'show-house' interiors and £20,000 kids tree houses like the Beckhams, there is at least one throwback to less architecturally-obsessed times. Ewan Cameron rented out his refurbished eco-friendly house in Edinburgh to Hearts' Phil Stamp but after only a few months was shocked to discover, as Scotland on Sunday reported, that "the place was absolutely bogging, with every carpet in the place ruined. We are only guessing what with, but it was minging." On his tour of inspection the landlord found "a bed was snapped in half and there was food actually on the ceiling. Curtains were pulled off, rails put up to hold jackets were hanging off the walls and someone has managed to fag-burn all the soft fittings."

FOOTBALLERS' HOUSING CHECKLIST

A Only Surrey and Cheshire will really do. If you're unfortunate to play for a club more than a hundred miles away from these twin football oases, remember chartering a helicopter might be steep but it will save you the embarrassment of living in some unfashionable county and you'll recoup your expenses in equity.

B *Hello!, OK!* and MTV pay top whack for features on houses designed by ex-Bradford non-scoring strikers' wives and Iraq born businessmen. If Dawn Ward is too busy, why not see what Mrs Carboni can do with a seven-figure budget?

C If you have to live abroad, don't eschew the "games room" philosophy. Do what Steve McManaman, Michael Owen and Jonathan Woodgate did and get the UK racing channels on satellite subscription to give your den the requisite touch of Pontefract race track glamour.

D If you can't be arsed with getting off your vanilla leather 20-seater couch, give Andy Myers a ring. He could save you the trouble.

E Never let your house to a single football player.

FOOTBALLERS' DIY

Make your house a footballers' house with the handy
Balls! guide to home improvement, Premiership style...

The living room

It's all about the size of your flat screen, which needs to be
both absolutely enormous and not quite as big as the one in
your private cinema. Flat screens are extremely expensive –
but cheap and easy to mimic, at least while turned off.
Simply buy a large, rectangular canvas and paint it black.
Better still, buy a poster from Ikea and tell anyone who
comes round that it's only there to cover the plasma screen
while you're not watching it, as you think it looks a bit
garish. They might find this hard to believe, so you should
distract them by buying a fake leopard-skin sofa like Lee
Bowyer.

The bathroom

Michael Owen has a giant hot tub big enough to fit 10
people, but there's no need to go to such extremes. What
you do need is to convert your bathroom into a wet room.
You can do this instantly and cheaply simply by removing
the shower curtain.

The kitchen

Steve Stone has a giant wood-burning stove, but a traditional electric oven will probably get
the food hot just as well. More important is the television – in Harry Kewell's kitchen there's
a set that uses high-tech sensors to follow your movements around the room, so it's always
facing you when you want to watch it. Achieve the look for less by tying some string to the
base of your television and tying the other end round your neck. Jamie Redknapp's kitchen
has "lots of stainless steel, granite and walnut", according to his wife Louise. Stainless steel
and granite can be expensive, but walnuts can be purchased cheaply from your local
supermarket, especially in the run-up to Christmas.

The kids' room

Otherwise known as "the princess room", at least in Steven Gerrard's house. This differs from
traditional bedrooms only by being more pink and having a showpiece bed surrounded by
whispy material drapes. Easy to copy at home: a bit of repainting won't cost the earth, then
move the bed into the middle of the room and staple some net curtains to the ceiling. If they
are too pricey, you could always re-use the shower curtain here.

The master bedroom

This absolutely must have an en-suite bathroom. If you don't have one at the moment, and
there is no obvious space to put one in, consider installing a toilet in the wardrobe.

The pool

It can be terribly hard to decide what shape to make your pool in, and how to decorate it. Ryan Giggs has a Welsh dragon on the bottom of his; after what was apparently a heated argument, Coleen McLoughlin won the right to have the pool in the house she shares with Wayne Rooney decorated in pink. A mosaic of the couple was laid into the ceiling, with their initials underneath. Achieve the same look by re-installing the disgusting pink bath from the coloured suite that was in the house when you bought it, and sticking a polaroid of you and your loved one to the ceiling with Blu-Tac. The Rooneys also have a tannoy system so they can communicate with each other while in different areas of their mansion. Like them, you too could always hear when your name is called – and save a great deal of money – by ditching the tannoy system in favour of buying a much smaller house.

Interior decoration

A word of advice from Ian Walker's wife Suzi: "In terms of interiors, fake leopard skin, chintz and gold have had their day. Now it's all about clean-cut lines, with no clutter. Oh yeah, and loads of Buddhas."

Outside

Christmas is important, even if you've got a match to play on boxing day so you've got to miss *EastEnders* to go training. Some illumination would go down well here: Wayne Rooney and Coleen McLoughlin spent £50,000 last Christmas on twinkly lights to make their mansion in Prestbury look like a giant Santa's grotto. "They're like a mini Blackpool," said a "source". Phil Neville, meanwhile, spent £5,000 lining his drive in Rawtenstall, Lancashire, with Christmas trees which he lit up in royal blue at night. "The trees are the talk of the village," said a "neighbour". Achieve the same effect for less by buying blue, glittery artificial Christmas trees from Woolworths and coming out at half-hourly intervals through the night to shine a torch at them.

And if it all goes wrong

You can always demolish it. Wayne Rooney and Roy Keane both snapped up 1930s mansions only to knock them right down and start again. But not every Manchester-based footballer is quite so remorseless – Ryan Giggs is something more of a traditionalist, and couldn't bear to destroy everything he'd just bought. So when he spent £1.9m on a Victorian manor in Worsley he didn't knock it all down – he kept the sundial. Similarly, in case the insurers refuse to cough up for the house you've just reduced to rubble, make sure you keep the garden shed. You might be needing it.

Fabrice Fernandes
Bolton Wanderers

Signed: August 2005 from Southampton, free

Sold: January 2006 to Beitar Jerusalem, free

Born: 29 October 1979

Height: 5ft 9in

Bolton appearances: 5 (+2 as sub), 0 goals

Career appearances: 190 (+42 as sub), 14 goals

Reason we're putting in so many statistics: He hardly played any football. Despite being contracted to English league clubs for the whole of 2005, he started just two league games.

Top fact 1: He owns a Porsche Cayenne, the same car as Jens Lehmann.

Top fact 2: While at Fulham he once phoned the "player liaison officer" Mark Maunders demanding to know why he was regularly waking up with a wet head. The answer? He was leaving the window open, and sometimes it rained.

Random information: His last act of the 2005/06 season saw him kick a Hapoel Petah Tikva player in the last minute of Betar Jerusalem's final match and get sent off.

Marks out of 10: Passing 8; Technique 8; Wing Wizardry 8; Mystery Disappearances 8; Inexplicable Injuries 8.

A career in quotes

Sam Allardyce: "He has a sweet left foot and an abundance of skill. Being a left-sided player he is a rare commodity in the modern game. Once I heard he wasn't affiliated to a club, I moved quickly to bring him in."

Fernandes: "I am pleased to be joining such a progressive club. I've been training here for a couple of days and the talent and spirit in the camp was one of the main reasons why I decided to join."

Neil McCann: "A newspaper did a list of 10 players who, it was implied, were happy just to turn up and do nothing for their money. I was mentioned along with Fabrice Fernandes. I was hurt by that - and angered as well."

His agent: "Sam asked him if he wanted to go out on loan for a month to play. However, Fabrice prefers to wait for his chance at Bolton. He is ready to work hard to catch the eye of Sam Allardyce in training."

Allardyce: "Fernandes wants to go and I don't want players who don't want to stay here. As yet, we've had no enquiries."

THE HARD SELL

SCENE: Milan Mandaric and 'Arry are chatting on the dog & bone...

Milan Mandaric: "I hear you're not happy at St Mary's."

'Arry Redknapp: "I hear you're not happy at Fratton Park."

Mandaric: "No, but you'd have to be a statue not to weep with laughter at the job you've done over there."

Redknapp: "And touché my friend. Where's your Serbian director of football and French manager got you? Heading for the drop, that's where."

Mandaric: "And where's your 'irreplaceable Bald Eagle' got you? You actually went down and let the indispensable become dispensable."

Redknapp: "So what do you propose?"

Mandaric: "It seems your mission is accomplished over there, why don't you come back?"

Redknapp: "Once bitten, twice shy. What do you take me for?"

Mandaric: "Did I mention this Russian fella has just given me £20 million and you can have it to buy players. You can get whoever you want."

Redknapp: "Oh, I wonder if Titi Camara is available?"

Mandaric: "What?

Redknapp: "Er, sorry. You know you can be very persuasive. I think I might come back and we could have some fun, couldn't we?"

Mandaric: "Well, at the very least we could always laugh at Rupert Lowe."

Redknapp: "Sandra, I'm just popping out."

NOVEMBER

63

Oh, we live in a pineapple under the sea...

DECEMBER

Thieves stole £30,000 worth of jewellery from Cristiano Ronaldo's house in Woodford, Cheshire, including a collection of Cartier watches that had been loaned to the winger ... Doncaster Rovers' owner John Ryan announces that seeing his side beat Aston Villa in the Carling Cup was a "far, far bigger thrill" than seeing Melinda Messenger topless – his plastic surgery company Transform had been responsible for the model's breast enlargements ... Villa chairman Doug Ellis hits back by saying that the defeat was more painful than when he broke his neck – "and I spent 17 days in hospital when I did that" ... Boxer Ricky Hatton reveals that when footballers moan about their workloads he "laughs his c**k off". "The sacrifice a boxer makes is incomparable," he says ... John Terry is photographed making regular visits to his local branch of Ladbrokes in Esher, Surrey. "When you're on such colossal wages, a few grand here and there is like pocket money," says "a regular" – Jose Mourinho responds by saying that "an Englishman going to the bookmaker is normal. In every street I find a minimum of three bookmakers. That's your country. For me, John Terry betting is normal" ... Chocolate digestives were named Britain's all-time favourite biscuit, coming in just ahead of custard creams in a nationwide poll. Admittedly, this isn't strictly relevant to football outside the old "what's your favourite half-time snack" debate, but it's the type of information we all need ... Harry Kewell wrote to his wife Sheree Murphy while she was on reality TV show *I'm a Celebrity Get Me Out of Here*, pleading with her to stop embarrassing him. "Please stop telling the world I love the Backstreet Boys," he wrote. Other revelations included details about the smoothness of his bottom and his habit of spreading rose petals around their mansion when it's her birthday ... Paul Gascoigne is sacked as manager of Kettering Town after 39 days for being "under the influences of alcohol several times" ... Coleen McLoughlin insists she will still marry Wayne Rooney despite CCTV pictures of the England striker getting saucy in a kitchen with another woman at the Odyssey bar in Altrincham. "I've had my bad times and my good times but I'm enjoying it," she says ... Noel Gallagher delivers a sombre tribute to George Best, who died in November. "He transcended football. He owned a nightclub and a clothes shop, drove a Ferrari and shagged Miss World. The only thing he didn't do that was cool was play music, and he probably would have been good at that, too." ... Rafa Benitez compares defender Jamie Carragher to animated TV character Spongebob Squarepants, because of his ability to soak up pressure. "I know that name from when my children watch television," he explains … Getafe boss Bernd Schuster reveals what led to a televised row with David Beckham. "I wished him a Merry Christmas and a happy new year," he says. "He goes around looking for trouble. He has to change his attitude" … Peter Crouch ends his Liverpool goal drought by scoring against Wigan after 24 hours and 19 minutes of playing time for the Anfield club. Even then, it takes the FA's dubious goals committee to decide that the effort should be his and not credited to blundering goalie Mike Pollitt … Jimmy Floyd Hasselbaink says the area he grew up in was so tough he "would often see people killing themselves by jumping from tower blocks" … Arsenal release their own-brand cologne, describing "an exhilarating aroma that combines subtlety and staying power" … Manchester United finish bottom of their Champions League group after losing at Benfica, where Cristiano Ronaldo gives the fans a one-finger salute. "I was hot-headed," he says later. "I never wanted to disrespect anyone" … Liverpool investigate after a 2005 Champions League winners' medal is sold on ebay for £1,500 to a mystery bidder from Hong Kong … Jose Mourinho unveils his waxwork at Madame Tussauds … El-Hadji Diouf is banned from driving for a year and fined £3,000 after failing a drink-driving test, and despite his claims that he "only" drank three glasses of champagne and that it would be "inconvenient" for him to be banned because he's so famous … adidas unveil the new World Cup ball, to be called Teamgeist. They claim it is "softer" than previous versions. Heidi Klum takes charge of the World Cup draw, which pits England with Sweden again. "It's like a love affair between us," says their manager Lars Lagerback … Coleen McLoughlin is planning her own clothing range. "If the right offer came along I would definitely do it," she suggests … John Terry reveals his fiancee Toni Poole is expecting twins during the World Cup … Terry picks up the £30,000 bar tab at Chelsea's Christmas party at the Elysium nightclub, where reserve keeper Lenny Pidgeley smashes a mirror after the table he was dancing on gives way. "They are young boys," says Mourinho. "They have to do sometimes what others of their age like to do" … Charlton striker Jay Bothroyd drives his Porsche into a lamp post. A "source" says the former Serie A ace was "acting strangely and not very coherent", but the star says he simply "blacked out" … Jose Mourinho reacts with fury after an Arsenal underling checks whether the Chelsea Christmas card received by Arsène Wenger had actually been written by the special one. Sports minister Richard Caborn suggests they should "grow up" … Paolo di Canio is banned for one game for giving a Nazi salute to Lazio fans … Manchester United's Christmas party features a nativity play performed by members of the club's youth team, in which the baby was named Wayne and a pantomime horse was wearing a Van Nistelrooy shirt … Wenger comments on the Christmas card fiasco, in which Mourinho apologised for having previously called the Arsenal boss a "voyeur". "I appreciated the sentiments in the card," he said. "But if a card had come in or not come in, it would not change the way I feel. We got this card and we didn't make a fuss of it." So that's what happens when you don't make a fuss, then …

Tax-iiiii !!

Managers of the month
DECEMBER
Who won the awards:

PREMIERSHIP

Rafa Benitez (Liverpool)
Five games, five wins and one goal conceded is what's known as title-winning form. Well, if you do it over more than a couple of months it would be.

CHAMPIONSHIP

Nigel Worthington (Norwich)
Five wins from six games is right proper good form, and meant that the Canaries boss at least got some silverware from the season. Let's face it, they never looked likely to get anything else.

LEAGUE ONE

Ronnie Moore (Oldham)
Two draws and three wins – all of which by the same 2-1 scoreline. Now that's clever.

LEAGUE TWO

Paul Simpson (Carlisle)
They only won three of their five games, but they didn't lose any. Which is good enough to get Chris Kamara excited. "Paul deserves all the accolades," he said.

Who should have won the award:

Chris Coleman (Fulham)

He's always a friendly fellow, the Fulham manager, so you'd think that if anyone was likely to be full of festive fun at Christmas then Chris must. But the season does funny things to football folk. "I'm always grumpy at Christmas," Coleman said when asked to impart some festive spirit, adding: "I haven't even sent any cards this year."

Fired!

Obviously Harry Redknapp wasn't quite sacked, having returned to his former club Portsmouth in order to achieve a miracle recovery, but you catch the drift. Meanwhile Millwall are on to their third manager since the end of last season and bottom-of-the-league Stockport prove themselves entirely without seasonal cheer by dispensing with their boss just two days after Christmas.

Chris Turner (Stockport County)
Colin Lee (Millwall)
Mick Harford (Rotherham United)
Harry Redknapp (Southampton)

Hired!

Jim Gannon (Stockport County)
David Tuttle (Millwall)
George Burley (Southampton)
Harry Redknapp (Portsmouth)

STATISTICS

Top scorers (league only):

Ruud Van Nistelrooy (Man. Utd) – 15
Frank Lampard (Chelsea) – 12
Thierry Henry (Arsenal) – 10

So far this season
Most shots on target: **Wayne Rooney** (Man. Utd) – 41
Most shots off target: **Wayne Rooney** – 36
Most fouls without a booking: **Alexi Smertin** (Portsmouth) – 31
Most shots per goal: **Laurent Robert** (Portsmouth) – 37
Most offsides: **Darius Vassell** (Man. City) – 28

Match of the month

BENFICA 2 MANCHESTER UTD. 1

In which we discovered 1) Portuguese teams can beat British ones even without relying on Darius Vassell taking vital penalty kicks and even when they don't have the Special One as manager; 2) Ryan Giggs hates Cristiano Ronaldo – when he was substituted the Welsh wizard angrily demanded to be told why the winking winger was still on the pitch; 3) Cristiano Ronaldo hates Portuguese people, particularly Benfica fans – when he was substituted he showed them a single-fingered hand gesture of limited civility; 4) Manchester United players hate being substituted – when it happens they always get angry with someone.

Top of the table

		P	W	D	L	F	A	GD	Pts
1	CHELSEA	20	18	1	1	43	9	34	55
2	MANCHESTER UNITED	20	13	5	2	40	17	23	44
3	LIVERPOOL	18	12	4	2	26	9	17	40
4	TOTTENHAM	20	10	7	3	29	18	11	37
5	WIGAN ATHLETIC	20	11	1	8	25	24	1	34

Bottom of the table

		P	W	D	L	F	A	GD	Pts
16	EVERTON	20	6	2	12	11	30	-19	20
17	WEST BROM	20	5	4	11	19	29	-10	19
18	PORTSMOUTH	20	4	5	11	15	31	-16	17
19	BIRMINGHAM CITY	19	3	4	12	13	29	-16	13
20	SUNDERLAND	19	1	3	15	14	36	-22	6

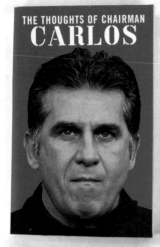

THE THOUGHTS OF CHAIRMAN
CARLOS

CARLOS QUEIROZ'S
FOOTBALL HANDBOOK
MODULE 5 – EUROPEAN FAILURE

❝ **SOME PEOPLES HAVE** little appreciation of football culture, and the Iberian peninsula is full of them. As I showed when I was in charge of Real Madrid, the anachronistic approach of some peers made it impossible for the highest echelons of defensive achievement to be rewarded in the requisite manner. Ronaldinho, the very antithesis of the Queirozian footballer, all shimmies and feints and let-the-defenders-look-after-themselves, wins awards which prioritise glitz over hits. He is lucky to have avoided Gary Neville, who is a superior being but like many great artists is doomed to be underappreciated in his own lifetime, a Rembrandt in red. My work in training was unflinching in its reach and we were ready for Benfica's system. I cannot be blamed for what followed. ❞

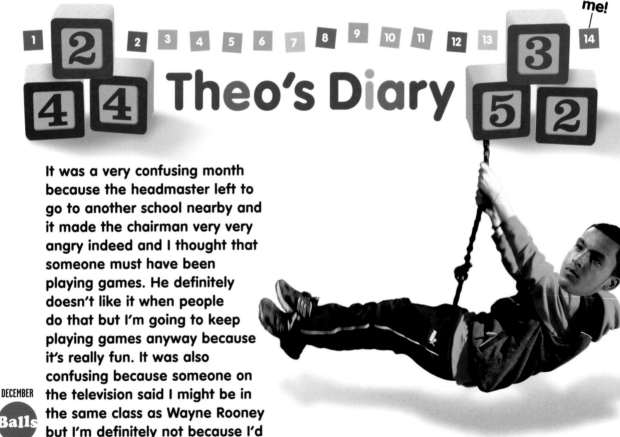

me!

1 2 2 3 4 5 6 7 8 9 10 11 12 13 3 14 4 4 5 2

Theo's Diary

It was a very confusing month because the headmaster left to go to another school nearby and it made the chairman very very angry indeed and I thought that someone must have been playing games. He definitely doesn't like it when people do that but I'm going to keep playing games anyway because it's really fun. It was also confusing because someone on the television said I might be in the same class as Wayne Rooney but I'm definitely not because I'd have seen him in maths.

Gordon Strachan's cheeseboard

Parmesan

A PROPER WINTER CHEESE. What you don't want is the type of cheese that goes all crumbly at this time of year, like caerphilly, and you don't want anything that's going to ooze uncontrollably at the sides like an over-ripe brie. You need something solid, something up front, something with guts. This is a workman's selection, you can taste the salt of its sweat and smell the pungent aroma of a sportsman's socks. It's got a dash of continental flair but it's still hard as nails, so it's going to be accepted by British cheese fans. It doesn't melt at high temperatures, and it's not going to freeze in the cold. It's a cheese for all seasons. Basically, it's great. Grated. It's great grated. I rate it when I ate it, it's impossible to hate it. I'm sorry, I appear to have started rapping.

Welcome to...
Middlesbrough

It might not be popular with all their signings but soon-to-be-released Brazilian midfielder Doriva was not immune to the charms of the north-east, and the country in general. Indeed, he was almost as fond of England as he was of repetition. "I love living in England," he said. "My children and my family love it here and I do not want to have to move them again. I am very happy here in England and I hope my future lies in Middlesbrough. If it doesn't, I really hope I am able to stay in England because I love it here." Thanks, mate. We get the message. Now get lost.

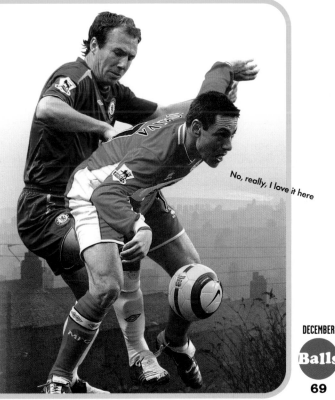

No, really, I love it here

I hate Christmas. The weather is cold, the Beaujolais is no longer nouveau, and the truffles are buried deep under the frozen ground. This is a time when people talk about goodwill to all men, yet they attempt to make my life a misery. There are too many games, too many training sessions, too many carol singers and far too many presents and cards.

Every year when I was a child I went to sleep in an empty room and woke up to find it full of presents, and not once did I hear the reindeers draw up with the sleigh, or wake to see Santa making his delivery. I think perhaps this was the first time I failed to see men wearing red doing conspicuous things that I really should have spotted, and I have been doing it ever since.

I care not for gifts. I have never received any at Arsenal in all my time there, and I never had any as a player. Thierry Henry, say, is gifted. He is fast, famous, charismatic, he has skills that I could only ever dream of. He has gifts. I never did. I hate gifts.

Patrick Vieira, say, got cards. Not just at Christmas but all year, every year. In fact, since I arrived at Arsenal my players have regularly received cards for all sorts of things. They receive all three types of cards: yellow cards, red cards and birthday cards. The Premier League appoint people whose very occupation is to give my players cards. For them, it is not even a hobby. But where are my cards? I never have any. I hate cards.

The likes of Wigan and Watford have goodwill. People like to see them do well because they are little clubs with an enterprising spirit. They have young managers who do not have the appearance of embittered history teachers. They saunter around the country attempting to rip up expectations and if they succeed they are applauded. On Match of the Day people who used to play for Liverpool coo and gurgle in pleasure. And what about my team? They are swift to criticise, ready to write us off, desperate to see us tumble. I have no good will, and never have. I hate goodwill.

I could keep going. I have thrown everything festive from my house. Sam Allardyce, like many Englishmen, has a collection of giant stockings, but I have thrown mine away. Chez moi, there will be no chestnuts roasting on the open fire, no mistletoe and only a bottle or two of wine. If someone accidentally sends me a present, I discard it. If the postman mistakenly delivers a card, I toss it aside. Do not try to suck me into your festive world, for I will be more likely to thumb my nose than shake your hand.

My job is to consider tactics, to ponder signings. For me Christmas is no more than the penultimate junction on the autoroute to the transfer window. People say I am cold, without joy. But I would rather be a man of ice that

"My first..."
Ronaldo

Double pie, mash and liquor, Oh all right, just one pie...

MY FIRST BREATH On 22 September 1976 I was born, inevitably, into terrible poverty in the favelas of Rio.

MY FIRST REASON TO HAVE A NICKNAME My full name is Ronaldo Luís Nazário de Lima, which is a bit of a mouthful.

MY FIRST NICKNAME O Fenômeno. It means the phenomenon, which is good I think.

MY FIRST WIFE was Milene Dominguez who was brilliant because she was the world champion of keepy-uppies. She managed 55,187 touches in just over nine hours, which is about as much football as I play in an average season.

MY FIRST SON was born in 2000. I was a bit busy with other stuff at the time so didn't have time to think of a new name and just called him Ronald.

MY FIRST WIFE WHO WASN'T BETTER THAN ME AT FOOTBALL was Daniella Cicarelli, an MTV VJ. It didn't last though – she wasn't happy when she had a miscarriage and instead of going to console her I went and played golf. This made me think that maybe I should keep my diamond rings to myself in future.

MY FIRST WORLD CUP WIN came in 1994, though I didn't play at all and I was only 17.

MY FIRST PROPER WORLD CUP WIN came in 2002, when I scored twice in the final and won the golden boot despite everyone saying I was finished and also having the distraction of a haircut that looked like someone had shaved off all the hair I couldn't see, leaving just the bit at the front that you can see in a mirror, and I hadn't noticed.

MY FIRST FATHER FIGURE (EXCEPT MY FATHER) was Sir Bobby Robson of England. "With him you can talk about anything and he has the ability to put a smile on your face. He is a fantastic man," I said once. He still couldn't make me sign for Newcastle, though.

MY FIRST BIG BELLY What do you mean belly? I'm not fat. People who say I'm fat are idiots. "People make mistakes when they call me fat," I said once. And I was right.

MY FIRST LESSON FOR THE KIDS OF TOMORROW As I said about my friend Ronaldinho, "I hope he has learned from me in terms of marketing strategy, my way of being and the way I play the game." In that order.

THE HARD SELL

SCENE: Peter Crouch and the Dubious Goals Committee

DGC: So, Peter, that was your goal then was it?

Crouchy: Yes, sir. Absolutely sir. One of my best, as it happens. And if you don't believe me you ask Rafa Benitez, because he's my manager and he said I scored it and he's the gaffer and he's always right.

DGC: From where we're sitting, which as you can see is frightfully close to the TV screen that is showing continuous slow-motion replays of the goal in question, it looks like the Wigan keeper had a hand in it.

Crouchy: Yes sir, but I had a foot in it and it's football isn't it so my foot beats his hand. If it was handball then it would be his goal. It's like scissors, paper, stone. Foot beats hand. Head beats hand. Hand's basically not very good, unless you're Didier Drogba but I don't think he plays by the same rules as the rest of us. So my hand couldn't beat my foot. Come to think of it, my hand couldn't even reach my foot, but I'm not sure that's the point.

DGC: So you kicked the ball, but then it hits someone else, totally changes direction, loops into the air towards the arms of the Wigan keeper, whose name I forget, and he's really in charge of the situation at that point.

Crouchy: Pollitt, sir.

DGC: Pull it, push it, punch it, you're right Peter – he could have done anything. But instead he flaps at it weak-wristedly …

Crouchy: I'm not sure weak-wristedly's a word, sir.

DGC: … and the ball loops up and into the net. Isn't that what happened Peter?

Crouchy: Not at all, sir. You see what happened is that the gaffer said if I just believe in myself then my luck will change. So I kept believing. And I was believing when I hit the shot, and it was the strength of my belief that sent the ball looping into the air, and it was the power of my positive thoughts that bemused the keeper, and it was the wonder of my wellbeing that carried the ball over the line, so it was my goal from beginning to end.

DGC: So we should give you the goal because you think we should? Is that the only reason?

Crouchy: To give is positive, sir. To take away is negative.

DGC: Oh, just take the sodding goal and get out of here.

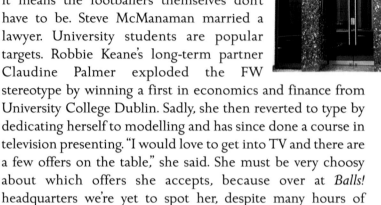

Romance

(Continued from p.35)

5. Clever things

Some FWs are really clever. This is helpful, as it means the footballers themselves don't have to be. Steve McManaman married a lawyer. University students are popular targets. Robbie Keane's long-term partner Claudine Palmer exploded the FW stereotype by winning a first in economics and finance from University College Dublin. Sadly, she then reverted to type by dedicating herself to modelling and has since done a course in television presenting. "I would love to get into TV and there are a few offers on the table," she said. She must be very choosy about which offers she accepts, because over at *Balls!* headquarters we're yet to spot her, despite many hours of gormlessly sitting in front of the television in the name of research. Like Palmer, Robin Van Persie's wife Bouchra studied economics. "She is a good girl," he says, and if that kind of praise isn't worth a few year's dedicated study we don't know what is.

6. Work out

Coleen McLoughlin, she of the workout videos, is the ultimate example of this. "My whole body has become really toned thanks to regular gym workouts," she says. "I reckon exercise is the key to looking and feeling good."

7. Award-winning art

Not such a common one this, but Susan Gunn, wife of the former Norwich and Scotland goalkeeper Bryan Gunn, won the 25,000-Euro Sovereign Art Prize last year for a huge red painting called Specto Spectus I & II. The judges praised the work as "a carmine-coloured painting whose subtle surface textures speak of an overt male world of leather-bound clubs, but also a subversive powerful female reality that links it to blood and veins which appear to work below the surface".

8. Talk about other footballers' wives

As in: "Victoria Beckham's so fake. I think she inspired the show Footballers' Wives with her pretend lifestyle, but it's not like that for the rest of us. She pushes that image." That's Sheree Murphy. See also: "The last time I was in Cricket, Alex and Coleen were in there. They're really nice girls." That's her too.

WHERE TO FIND A GIRL

1. A nightclub

History suggests there is no better place to find a FW. Footballers from Ashley Cole to Nacho Novo have settled down with women they found while out clubbing. So frequently are footballers to be found womanising at top nightspots we've dedicated a whole section (The Good Nightclub Guide, page 28) to the subject. We suggest you look there later, if you haven't already, for some more voyeuristic fun.

2. A beauty contest

Robbie Keane's belle Claudine Palmer is a former Miss Ireland finalist while football groupie Leilani is a former Miss Great Britain. But Teddy Sheringham is the ultimate example of this method, having judged the Miss GB contest in 2005 – and then immediately got to work on romancing the winner. In fact, he didn't even wait until the contest was over, asking her during the event who her favourite footballer was. "You, of course," she replied. "Well you're definitely my number one," he said. Simple, a

little bit sad, but despite the 18-year age difference it worked: the veteran striker was seen "kissing the face off her" at the after-show party at trendy nightspot Pangaea. The pair shared a couple of dates before the beauty queen, Danielle Lloyd, told the press about what she had planned for their next meeting. "I'd cook up my favourite meal – steak and chips and champagne. As an hors d'oeuvre I'd wear my sexiest lingerie in the kitchen while making the food just to get him going. Then I'd serve him something special for dessert – me! I wouldn't rule out doing it on the dining room table." We were unable to find out if, like Sven, he insisted on loading the dishwasher first.

3. A brothel

The less said about this the better, eh Wayne?

4. School

Footballers know of only two types of relationship. There's the "childhood romance", and there's the one that begins in a nightclub. Michael Owen was on the look-out for women with marital potential at a particularly early age, having met his future wife Louise when they were still at junior school. Manchester United's strikers have a youth policy of their own, as both Wayne Rooney and Ruud van Nistelrooy, who met his wife Leontien Slaats when he was still in short trousers, were with their current partners by the time they left school. And Ruud van Nistelrooy is still in short trousers. (Continued p.98)

Pro-Licence Examination

The League Managers' Association ruled that without a Uefa Pro Licence Glenn Roeder could manage Newcastle United on a caretaker basis for 12 weeks only. But we at *Balls!* are prepared to step in and sanction his appointment on a long-term basis if he can pass our only slightly less prestigious written exam for budding managers. Get a pen Glenn…

1. As a manager your primary responsibility is to
- a) The fans
- b) The chairman
- c) Yourself

2. Is your football philosophy
- a) To entertain at all costs
- b) To win at all costs
- c) To save your job at all costs

3. Your preferred system is
- a) 4-2-4
- b) 4-4-2
- c) 4-5-1

4. Your star player gives an interview in which he talks about his concerns about the club Do you:
- a) Read the interview in full, ask him for the context of his comments and address them
- b) Fine him two weeks wages and ring up a friendly journalist to tell him the severity of the reprimand using the phrase "in no uncertain terms"
- c) Ban him from the training ground and sell him within 24 hours for half his true value

5. One of your players scythes down an opponent in a two-footed tackle from behind in front of the referee and is sent off. Do you
- a) Claim the player will be disciplined by your club
- b) Claim you did not see the incident so couldn't possibly comment
- c) Claim there's a vendetta against your club

6. A scout sends you a video of a player he's representing with a view to him signing for your club. Do you:
- a) Tell him you have your own scouts to recommend transfer targets
- b) Watch the video and make an assessment
- c) Sign him up and ask whether the agent has any jobs going for your nephew

7. You would like to sign a player who is under contract to a rival team. Do you:
- a) Telephone the manager and ask if he would be prepared to transfer the player?
- b) Tell the player's agent of your interest and make sure the newspapers know too
- c) Invite him to come and visit your facilities, show him around, tell him how much he can expect to earn from your club, buy his mother a yacht and see if anyone does anything about it

8. Your match day apparel of choice:
- a) Depends on the weather
- b) An Italian tailored overcoat and suit
- c) A suit when you're winning but a tracksuit when results have not been so good to emphasise how hard you've been working to sort it out

9. Your hero is:
- a) Bill Shankly
- b) Frank Sinatra
- c) Joseph Stalin

10. A broadcaster gives his verdict on your team's performance and it's not favourable. Do you
- a) Respect his right to give a professional opinion even if you disagree with it
- b) Confront him and argue your case
- c) Never speak to anyone who works for the same company ever again

Answers: All As: You're not cut out for this, have you considered a career in the church?
All Bs: Hard luck. You have qualified for our provisional diploma licence
All Cs: Congratulations. Just send a postal order for £9.99 and you will receive a *Balls!* Official Pro Licence certificate by return of post.

Nightclubs

Continued from p.48

ELYSIUM, LONDON

68 Regent Street W1B 5EL / Tel. 020 7439 7770

Latin for "place of the blessed", Elysium is built on the site of a former Masonic temple. It's slightly easier to get into these days, though entrance to the VIP rooms is a little more difficult.

Tabloid tales

This is where Chelsea's reserves hang out, or so it seems. Admittedly, the whole team turned up as part of the title-winning party in 2005, when they swiftly ran up a £30,000 bar tab (paid in full by John Terry) and caused further problems when reserve keeper Lenny Pidgeley smashed a giant mirror when the table he was dancing on collapsed under his weight. Happier to be under his weight was Big Brother "babe" Orlaith McAllister, seen "snuggling up" to the Pidgemeister here. Glen Johnson was seen to have "exchanged phone numbers" with model Leilani (who ended up getting engaged to Arsenal's Jeremie Aliadière). Arsenal's Quincy Owusu-Abeyie was allegedly involved in a fight in the reception area here in April 2005, after the PFA player of the season awards. He spent 16 hours in custody.

EMBASSY, LONDON

29 Old Burlington Street, Mayfair, W1S 3AN
Tel. 020 7851 0956 / www.embassylondon.com

Where the VIP room overlooks the dancefloor, for ideal "I'll-have-that-one" celebrity girl-spotting. "Perfect for the modern-day voyeur", they suggest.

Tabloid Tales

Joe Cole demonstrated his mastery of seduction in March when he approached someone who vaguely resembled a member of All Saints, said: "I love your group, can I sing with you?" and promptly launched into an unedifying rendition

of the Dad's Army theme tune, 'Who Do You Think You are Kidding, Mr Hitler'. That really happened. We didn't make it up. John Terry, who was also there that night, performed a striptease in the VIP room after victory over Huddersfield in January. Also there were Rio and Anton Ferdinand, Bobby Zamora, Jeremy Aliadière, Teddy Sheringham and Arjen Robben. Sheringham was once seen "being pursued by female fans" outside the club. Jermaine Pennant held his 23rd birthday party here, with Ledley King and Kieran Richardson among the football stars in attendance. Less impressively, Harry Kewell turned up when former *EastEnders* "star" Sid Owen held his 34th. This is where Cole and Anton Ferdinand met Page 3 model Keeley on the night that ended with Cole nursing a black eye and doing a runner from Keeley's parents' house without his socks. Ashley Cole and Cheryl Tweedy are regulars – he was once seeing "leering down his lover's cleavage as they left".

TRAP, LONDON

201 Wardour Street, W1 / Tel. 020 7434 3820
www.traplondon.com

"The brainchild of Fran Cosgrove", they proudly announce, a surprise for anyone who saw the man himself in *Celebrity Love Island* a couple of years back and had no idea that he was capable of brainchildren. The upshot is "a spacious, classic American warehouse-style bar" with "a chic and vibrant atmosphere".

Tabloid Tales

John Terry was seen snogging topless model Linsey Dawn McKenzie here, while this is where Graham Stack picked up the girl who later – unsuccessfully – accused him of rape.

Continued p.89

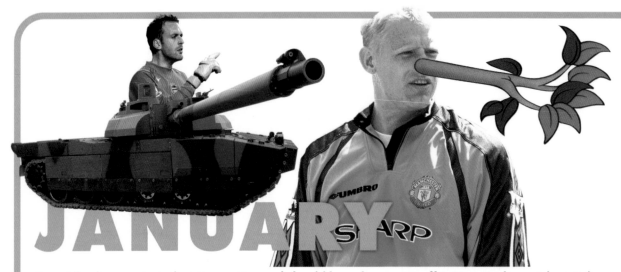

JANUARY

Sam Allardyce protests that Steven Gerrard should have been sent off in Liverpool's match at Bolton for stamping on Kevin Nolan but Gerrard denies he would ever break the Liverpudlian code of honour: "Kevin's a good scouser. Why would I ever deliberately try to hurt him?" ... He may literally have a level head in the fact that you could successfully rest a sack of parsnips on top of it but does this mean that Pascal "another yellow card for Arsenal's fifth choice centre-half" Cygan should offer advice on controlling one's emotions on the field? Or does his meaning go deeper? Whatever, this is one mean way to sum up England's premier occasionally-injured striker: "Wayne's weak point is his brain" ... Patrick Vieira reveals his real reason for leaving Arsenal: "I left London as there was nothing left to stimulate me" ... Frank Lampard feels no sadness at the reaction he gets from West Ham fans though he thinks his father, "a Hammer through and through" would not have liked the Upton Park's rendition of "You're just a fat Paul Ince" at his son during Chelsea's victory ... An employee at the Co-op Bank in Manchester is jailed for his part in the theft of £323,000 from the accounts of former City players Daniel van Buyten, Vincent Vuoso and Djamel Belmadi, though as they cost City £3.5m in transfer fees and an estimated £3m in wages for 13 appearances between them makes one ponder the meaning of robbery ... Sam Allardyce joins Sir Alex Ferguson in boycotting interviews with the BBC ... Nigel Clough and his Burton squad are keen to endorse locally-based Bovril before their cup tie with Manchester United and are photographed swilling piping cups of the curiously famous cow-flavoured beverage ... Leyton Orient beat Fulham in the Cup at Craven Cottage and Os' boss Martin Ling goes home on the tube ... Alan Shearer might not win anything at Newcastle United but who cares? He justifies his in no way selfish decision to play on for another year by equalling Jackie Milburn's scoring record for the club and Shay Given calls for a Shearer statue to be erected in the Toon ... Joe Cole is assaulted at a party at Page 3 stunna Keeley's house. He is forced to climb out of a window sockless at 5.30am to escape the attack, alleged to have been mounted by the serial breast exhibitor's partner. The answer to England's left-side problem™ turned up at the Near and Far minicab office covered in cuts, distinctly trousered but without shirt or shoes and desperate to arrange a ride-now-pay-later trip home ... Peter Schmeichel's *Match of the Day* punditry contract is terminated by the BBC apparently because of uninspired comments and stilted delivery rather than to save on flesh-tone powder for his vermillion hooter … Portsmouth sign striker Benjamin Mwaruwari, though trusting someone known as 'The Undertaker' with resurrecting your chances of survival seems ill advised … Hernan Crespo feels that if Chelsea's owner picked the team he would be a regular. "Roman Abramovich worships me," he modestly says … Sheffield United buy 90% stake in Chinese club Chengdu Five Bull … On *Celebrity Big Brother* Faria Alam alleges that the FA would like to have hanged her for selling the story of her and Sven's romance to the *News of the World*. But she remains convinced that she and the Swede were genuinely "in love" … In an astonishing pre-Manchester derby pot and kettle fest Sir Alex Ferguson says City's new ground is "quiet. You don't get the same atmosphere as you do at Old Trafford". Presumably he means the constant rustling of superstore bags … Auxerre's Abou Diaby admits he chose Arsenal over Chelsea because "Wenger was better than Mourinho, that's all". That's all? Fifteen months of tabloid rivalry dismissed in two words … Sven-Goran Eriksson falls for the charms of "fake sheikh" Mazher Mahmood and is so flattered he ends up agreeing to manage Aston Villa … he also promises to recruit David Beckham to sell claret and blue strips and excuses Wayne Rooney's recklessness by saying "he's just a small boy from a small family" … Ruud van Nistelrooy and Cristiano Ronaldo have to be pulled apart after a classic "training ground bust-up". According to eyewitness reports the Dutchman, annoyed at Ronaldo's showboating, told him that he'd "achieved nothing, absolutely nothing" and then stormed off the pitch. Another player shouted after him: "Look at Ruud – he's stomping off like a 10-year-old kid." Next week, the children of Old Trafford will be playing doctors and nurses … More bad news for Manchester United as all their kit is stolen on the night before their trip to Manchester City. They lose 3-1 … El-Hadji Diouf is fined £550 for pushing the former Bolton player Khalilou Fadiga's ex-wife … "A little bit of naivety has crept in," says Alan Curbishley on Sven's predicament. "He'll live and learn." Don't bet on it … Emmanuel Adebayor arrives at Arsenal and takes Kanu's former number, 25. "This really is an honour for me," he says. "Kanu is my idol" … Roman Abramovich injures his knee playing football with his kids. Four minders accompany him for a scan at the Wellington Hospital … Wayne Rooney completes a safe driving course … Manuel Almunia has time on his hands since Jens Lehmann's resurgence last year and explains he's spent it wisely: "I am fascinated by World War II," he says, "Panzer tanks and Spitfires. I've got lots of photos of my trips to the Imperial War Museum". Bet Jens is pleased … Rio Ferdinand is sent off after fouling Robbie Savage in the second Carling Cup semi second leg but Gary Neville tries to pin the blame on the Rovers midfielder, at least until he is silenced and sent on his way by former team-mate Mark Hughes: "You have always got something to say, you have," says the Blackburn manager in the tunnel with a precision that brooks no quibble. "Why don't you shut the fuck up?" …

A word in your shell-like, Mr. E…

Managers of the month
JANUARY

Who won the awards:

PREMIERSHIP
David Moyes (Everton)
Beating Arsenal and drawing with Chelsea is good enough for Nic Gault of Barclays to hand the award to soccer's sunniest manager. "Moyes and his team have really started to turn things around," he says.

CHAMPIONSHIP
Billy Davies (Preston North End)
What do they put in the water in Preston, where Moyes also cut his manager's teeth. Was it tranquilisers? Making it a double for morose Scots, the thesaurus-free Sky pundit Chris Kamara salutes North End's four straight wins in January: "Billy deserves all the accolades."

LEAGUE ONE
Phil Parkinson (Colchester Utd.)
Seven wins in the month, surmises Kamara, "was a fantastic achievement", leading him to conclude with unerring accuracy: "it just shows how consistent they have been in recent weeks."

LEAGUE TWO
Colin Calderwood (Northampton Town)
Capping a wonderful month for the Cobblers, in which he even managed to sign 34-year-old

ex-pineapple plinth Jason Lee, the man who was spun dizzy by Ronaldo in the opening game of the 1998 World Cup finals is the beneficiary of Kamara's exceptional insight. "His side," he concludes, "seem more determined than ever to secure an automatic promotion place this season."

Who should have won the award:
Graeme Souness (Newcastle Utd.)
Two clean sheets with three of his back four comprising Boumsong, Babayaro and Bramble, the worst collection of bees since Michael Caine eluded The Swarm, is worth its weight in accolade gold.

Fired!
Do it too early in the month and you might have the new man knocking on your door looking to dabble in the transfer market. But leave the dead man walking in situ until the end of the month like these four and it will please your bank manager:

Leroy Rosenior (Torquay Utd)
Craig Levein (Leicester City)
Phil Brown (Derby County)
Mark Wright (Peterborough)

Hired!
Steve Bleasdale (Peterborough)
Terry Westley (Derby County)
John Cornforth (Torquay United)
Simon Grayson (Blackpool)

STATISTICS
Top scorers (league only):
Ruud Van Nistelrooy (Man. Utd) – 18
Thierry Henry (Arsenal) – 14
Frank Lampard (Chelsea) – 13

So far this season
Most shots on target: **Lampard** (Chelsea) – 51
Most shots off target: **Rooney** (Man. Utd.) – 48
Most fouls without scoring:
Rochemback (M'boro) – 38
Most offsides: **Crespo** (Chelsea) – 37
Most free-kicks won: **Boa Morte** (Fulham) – 68

Match of the month
ARSENAL 7 MIDDLESBROUGH 0

In which we discovered: 1) Yakubu can score goals but does little else and when his team gets drubbed he will go missing from match reports, unless of course you read one of the posh papers who still aren't sure if he's actually called Aiyegbeni; 2) If Aiyegbeni, sorry Yakubu, Hasselbaink and Viduka, combined wages £7m p.a. can't score against an Arsenal back four of Lauren, Djourou, Senderos and Cygan, Steve McClaren's prospects of succeeding Sven Goran-Eriksson should be minimal; 3) If your name is Bradley Jones and you've been waiting patiently for a chance in goal for three years, this week, perhaps, is not the ideal time for your manager to fall out with Mark Schwarzer. 4) Poor Cliff Bastin goes 40 years with an unbroken record only to see it chalked off twice in seven years; 5) Aston Villa must be a pretty poor side if a only a defeat to them three weeks after a seven-goal drubbing makes you realise you've hit rock bottom. 6) There's no limit to the amount of times an "oh-0-7" headline can be wheeled out every time this unusual scoreline crops up.

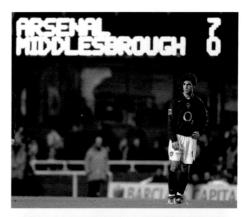

Top of the table

		P	W	D	L	F	A	GD	Pts
1	CHELSEA	24	20	3	1	50	13	37	63
2	MANCHESTER UNITED	24	14	6	4	45	24	21	48
3	LIVERPOOL	22	13	6	3	30	13	17	45
4	TOTTENHAM	24	11	8	5	31	20	11	41
5	WIGAN ATHLETIC	24	12	2	10	29	30	-1	38

Bottom of the table

		P	W	D	L	F	A	GD	Pts
16	MIDDLESBROUGH	23	6	7	10	30	40	-10	25
17	WEST BROM	24	6	5	13	21	32	-11	23
18	BIRMINGHAM CITY	23	5	5	13	21	32	-11	20
19	PORTSMOUTH	24	4	6	14	17	40	-23	18
20	SUNDERLAND	23	2	3	18	17	43	-26	9

THE THOUGHTS OF CHAIRMAN
CARLOS

CARLOS QUEIROZ'S
FOOTBALL HANDBOOK
MODULE 6 – A ROTATED CENTRE-FORWARD IS A HAPPY CENTRE-FORWARD

"THE BURDEN FOR SCORING goals falls, so the uninitiated believe, on the centre-forward. But this is too simplistic. Yes, our centre-forward is currently the Premiership's leading scorer but his glory-seeking habit is only the cherry on the cake of our creative play. And sometimes you don't want cherries on your cakes. If we live on a diet of cherry cakes, yes we will feel full, but our palates will become jaded as we yearn for something different - chocolate shavings, coconut sprinkles or candied peel. If we let the cherry dictate to the cake, the cherry will feel it is the most important ingredient and this cannot be good for cake morale. Instead we should rotate our toppings, bringing in something less expensive but just as likely to offer sustenance and bring out the best in the other flavours. Of course, the cherry will start to feel undervalued but for the overall good of the bun it needs occasionally to be sacrificed. Tell it that cherry cakes are not appropriate for all competitions and you will put it back on the menu when you see fit. You are the Jane Asher and your word goes. What's it going to do, demand to leave your bakery and move to some fancy patisserie? I don't think so."

me!

Theo's Diary

I was having a really good month and I scored a goal in the cup competition and we won but they still wouldn't give us the cup which I thought was very mean. I was quite upset and then things got even worse when a new French teacher arrived and said I had to change schools and go and live away from mum and dad in this big place with lots of people in that he called l'oendun but I haven't learned that word in French yet. There might be a circumflex on the u I never know when there should be one of them.

JANUARY

Balls

82

Gordon Strachan's cheeseboard
Dubliner

I LOVE A BARGAIN truckle and, matured over 37 years, this is one of my all-time favourites. I enjoyed its versatility at Coventry but its smooth, industrious and ineffably sweet-natured texture was a luxury I could not afford at Southampton. But here it comes absolutely free and its "yes boss", "can-do" approach to filling a hunger gap is exactly what you need when a rival manager, say Steve Bruce, nicks another vintage cheese off your after-dinner platter. The cheese bears the name of the Irish capital and has a light tang that soothes the nerves like a Kenny G sax break. To enjoy it at its best, keep it on wood – a block, or perhaps a bench – for around 60 minutes then tuck in. There's definitely no hairs on this one and I am happy to see it win its first medal after 18 years' shunting around the lesser cheese boards of England.

Welcome to... Glasgow

Shunsuke Nakamura Celtic's £2.7m summer signing from Reggina originally lived alone in Glasgow, waiting for the arrival of his wife and infant son (built, he terrifyingly admits, "like John Hartson" – the son, that is). Amid a string of compliments about the city and its culture he admits that the weather in Scotland "may be a bit cold and wet" but then tries to wriggle out of it by adding "but I'm pleased to be here", even though he has to import his own rice because "rice from Japan is more substantial than the rice you get here." Alright Shunsuke, you may go on, improbably, to praise Irn Bru, "I tried a can and must admit I liked it", show such respectful courtesy that when questioned about the national dish you said, "Haggis? Is that a type of sausage? I eat absolutely anything so I am sure I will try it sometime," and claim the city "is a very nice place to live and I feel I can be comfortable here." But what about the poor downtrodden labourers of the paddy fields of East Kilbride? Think of the damage your comments about puny rice has on them. Do you have no compassion?

Balls investigates...
THE ENVIRONMENT

WE ARE ALL being encouraged to consider the environmental implications of our actions, but it seems that football – and certainly footballers – are scrimping on the scrutiny. Other than recycling managers, they seem happy to fritter away our natural resources so it falls to us to turn the spotlight onto our eco-shy heroes.

Take, for example, Wayne Rooney. When his broken metatarsal was threatening to keep him out of the World Cup he at one stage flew to Germany and back and back again within three days, the last two journeys on board a private jet. In the circumstances it was hardly surprising when, later in the competition, Coleen decided she needed a haircut and chose to have it performed in Liverpool. Another rapid return flight beckoned. With all of that travelling and the resulting emissions you start to wonder how they sleep at night (sadly we know the answer, as revealed in Rooney's autobiography – by leaving the lights, the television, the hairdryer and the hoover running).

Perhaps the forward can talk about his ecological footprint with David Beckham, whose own footprint is created using a new pair of adidas Predator boots every time he plays, each of them fashioned out of the finest kangaroo leather. We know there are a lot of very fine kangaroos in Australia, but that's a whole lot of bouncy marsupial.

The list of questions goes on: why turn on the floodlights five hours before kick-off?

Has anyone ever seen a Premiership footballer on public transport? Does Sir Alex Ferguson's famous hairdryer treatment have any negative environmental implications? Does it make Rooney fall asleep?

But the villain of this piece is not Rooney or Beckham or Ferguson, but an unassuming Spaniard who plays for Bolton. Unassuming, but very fussy when it comes to his hair.

In June 2006 Ivan Campo signed a new two-year contract at Bolton, and ecologists worldwide wept. It is, you see, the Spaniard's habit to, Coleen-style, return home for his haircuts. Every three weeks he flies from Manchester to Madrid for no reason other than to have his locks trimmed, and then returns to the bosom of Big Sam looking, frankly, indistinguishable from the curly-haired scruff who first departed.

"Ivan is really precious about his hair," a "source" told the *Sun* last year. "For as long as he's had long hair he's had the same hairdresser. He flies from Manchester to Madrid every three weeks to get a haircut. His boss Sam Allardyce doesn't mind so long as he's back for training."

Let's do the maths. The Spaniard first signed for Bolton in August 2002. Four seasons with the club equates to roughly 196 weeks. Take out five weeks each year for the close season, when Campo presumably relocates to an area with more convenient access to his hairdresser, and we're left with 181 weeks. With a haircut every third week, that's 60 return trips, adding up to 172,200km – equivalent to the entire public road network of the Ukraine (there's a fact you'll never need again).

The icecaps are melting and a solution must be found but as with all complicated issues, there is no easy answer. There is, however, an obvious place to start: with Ivan Campo, a Mancunian barber and some hard-wearing shears. And Coleen, you're next.

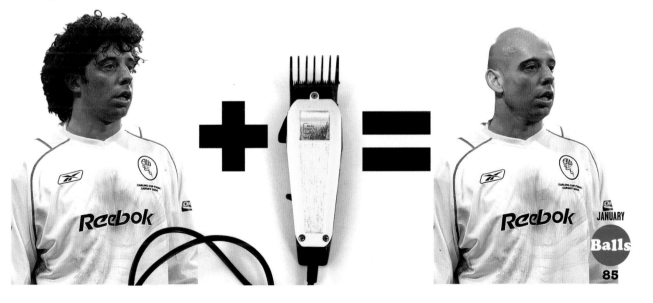

Per Kroldrup
Everton

Date of birth: 31 July 1979

Bought for: £5.1m from Udinese in June 2005

Sold for: £3.6m to Fiorentina in January 2006

Total English league experience:
One game against Aston Villa on Boxing Day 2005.
Everton lost 4-0

Pounds lost by Everton on his value per minute he spent on the pitch: £10,205

Irrelevant fact: His favourite band are Nick Cave and The Bad Seeds – "A bit dark, not a reflection of what I'm like."

Interesting fact: Arsenal almost bought him in 2001

Marks out of 10: Bench-warming 9;
Seat-in-Stand Warming 9; Team-sheet Bothering 2

A career in quotes

June 2005: "The club appeals to me and the Premiership would be an interesting place to play. I want to enjoy the best part of my career here at Everton."

David Moyes, July 2005: "He's a bit of a risk because he is an unknown in terms of playing in the Premiership. But he's young, enthusiastic and keen to improve."

November 2005: "It is frustrating sitting it out when you are used to playing every week."

David Moyes, November 2005: "He's taken a while to settle in, perhaps a little longer than expected, and we have had to work on a few things."

December 2005: "Hopefully, with the number of games over Christmas, my chance will come."

A week later: "I would really like to return to Italy. I don't really feel I have had the chance to prove my worth."

Fiorentina sporting director Pantaeleo Corvino: "We have always said that Fiorentina would continue to look for quality in the transfer market and the acquisition of Per Kroldrup must be seen as that."

March 2006: "I still believe I could have done well in the Premiership but in Italy there's more emphasis on technical skills. I am used to coaches and fans who prefer that you play yourselves out of trouble and pass to a team-mate."

THE HARD SELL

SCENE: Rafa and Robbie chatting

Benitez: I think I need another striker.

Fowler: I'm your man.

Benitez: Hang on a minute. I haven't got any money to spend.

Fowler: I'm less than cheap. I'm free.

Benitez: Right. But there's always the wages. We sold you for £11m, then you went on to City for £6m. We can't afford the sort of salary that goes with transfer fees like that.

Fowler: I'll put my rents up and take a pay cut.

Benitez: Yes but then there's the length of contract. I can't go around burdening myself with financial commitments that might come back to bite me on the bum in a couple of years if it doesn't work out.

Fowler: I'll only come on trial, and if it works out great, if not, no hard feelings.

Benitez: But you won't be first choice and that's why you left under Houllier.

Fowler: But you're not Houllier.

Benitez: So you'll come for nothing, accept peanuts for wages, leave in six months if I want you to and be happy to play fourth fiddle to Morientes, Crouch and Cisse if that's what I decide?

Fowler: Yes. I'd crawl on my hands and knees to Liverpool if that's what it takes to make this transfer happen.

Benitez: Funny you should mention that ... alright, come home la'

JANUARY

Balls

87

ON THE ANALYST'S COUCH WITH
TONY ADAMS

Thierry Henry: "I don't know whether I'm coming or going. I feel abandoned by my friend Patrick and wonder if travel might broaden my mind. But, then again, I do like it here and I also feel responsible for these kids and they want me to stick around. What should I do?"

Big Tone: "This indecision's bugging you. If they don't want you, they should set you free. Exactly who are you supposed to be? Do they know which clothes even fit you? Come on and let me know. Should you cool it or should you blow?"

Thierry: "Aren't those the lyrics to a Clash song?"

Big Tone: "Err, insight comes from a variety of influentials. But I will take an empirical state building approach. You have a fear of abandoning people and one of being abandoned. It is called the "reluctant abandoner's fear of abandonment". We mentalist managers seek closure for the complex by deep foraging in your memory receptacle and ruling out confabulation. Then it's like "congratulations, you have no confabulation" and resolution begins. Deep psychosomanambuance emprobement is like taking a Rennie for your soul disorders. It calms the brain bubbles and healing begins. So, tell me about your childhood."

Thierry: "No offence, but I haven't got time for this."

Big Tone: "Willie. It's one for you."

Willie Young: "How much they offerin'?"

Thierry: "One has put £120,000 a week down, the other £130,000."

Willie Young: "There's not much to choose is there. Toss a coin."

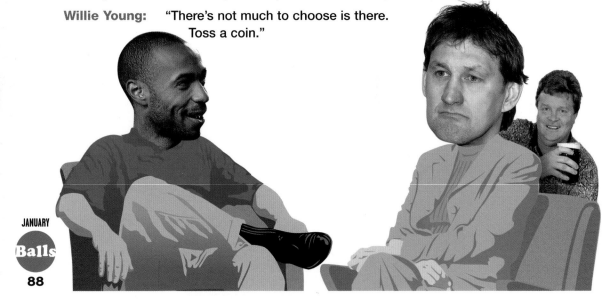

Nightclubs

Continued from p.77

MO*VIDA, LONDON

8-9 Argyll Street, W1F 7TF / Tel. 020 7734 5776
www.movida-club.com

"The most significant and exquisite club venue in London", they boast, where the VIP room is packed with velvet divans and sponsored by Dom Perignon. If you're hungry, they offer only slightly confused Franco-Anglo-Italian cuisine.

Tabloid Tales

Carlton Cole DJ'ed here after the FifPro Awards in September 2005, his appreciative crowd including Ashley Cole and William Gallas. This is also one of the venues that Cristiano Ronaldo passed through on his controversial night out in 2005, after Manchester United's 3-2 win over Fulham, that ended in an unsuccessful rape allegation. It will probably be best remembered, though, for hosting Glenn Johnson's late-night table dancing in March 2006. The next day he missed Chelsea's flight to their Champions League game in Barcelona after losing his passport. "At 2.45am he stood up on a table with glasses of champagne and vodka in both hands," says a "source".

SEONE, LONDON

41-43 St Thomas Street, SE1 3QX
Tel. 020 7407 1617

Under the arches of London Bridge station, a 3,000-capacity superclub exists. Being very big, it tends to scare away celebrity clients unless they can be absolutely sure that there will be other celebrity clients there to hang out with them. Hopefully by the time you read this they will have found a solution to the flooring problems in the main toilet block that were bothering them so earlier in the year.

Tabloid tales

Only one: Freddie Ljungberg came to the Alexander McQueen party last September.

FIFTY, LONDON

50 St James's Street SW1A 1JT
www.fiftylondon.com

If other London nightspots set managers' alarm bells ringing, this one is in another league of scariness. Good food, fine cocktails, beautiful people and late nights can be found anywhere, but "excellent private gambling facilities" coupled with "four floors of sophisticated, upscale bars and restaurants" and a club lounge, Fifty Below, feeds too many addictions to be at all healthy. First opened in 1827, so doing well to be fashionable.

Tabloid Tales

A member's club (annual membership just £750), this place doesn't divulge many secrets. But Frank Lampard was spotted last September.

Continued p.114

JANUARY

Balls

89

Nationality Test

Football is an international game, it breaks down borders. But at the same time it must live with them. This, to be frank, is a bit of a hassle. We want our teams to be full of the best young talent from around the world, but some Home Office functionary is employed to stop precisely that outcome. Instead, he will only stamp the passports of European journeymen and ageing internationals who have met the minimum qualifying standards for a work permit, which currently involve playing at least 138 internationals for one of the world's four best nations as ranked by Coca-Cola during the two weeks immediately preceding the application. Or something.

Work permits are no longer of any use. Their only point was to stop British clubs buying Ronaldinho until he became too rich and famous to want to play here anyway. Eventually, when he's 38 and approximately four years after he should have retired, he'll move to Bolton on a free transfer, where he will play brilliantly for six months before disappearing for the remainder of his contract, spotted intermittently sitting in the stands wearing designer sunglasses and clutching an entirely unnecessary Louis Vuitton washbag. This is not good for the game in this country. Both France and Spain have hosted Ronaldinho, while England got Henrik Pedersen. All we want is fairness.

The system must be changed to allow people to play in this country even when they are young, Brazilian, and don't have a forged Italian passport and a hastily-prepared backstory about a grandmother from the hills of Umbria. Being a footballer, good enough to samba his way into the nation's leading teams, is passport enough. Permits should be handed out by a team of talent-spotters based on a test of skills rather than parentage. One day, that Nike advert where the Brazil team played their way round an airport will be re-enacted on a regular basis at Heathrow as brilliant ball-jugglers touch down determined to prove themselves to a skill-hungry nation. Until then, however, we need a reliable way to sort out whether a supposed footballer is either any good or from the country's he says he is. May we propose this simple, footballing nationality check. Within 15 questions, we can tell a Brazilian from a Brummie and spot any Italian interlopers while we're at it.

1. A sprightly winger is sprinting down the byline towards a through-ball played into space by a midfielder. The full-back gets there just before the attacker. Should he:

   a) drag the ball back with his studs, confusing the attacker, before turning and playing the ball across the line to a centre-back with the outside of his right boot

   b) hit the ball into the onrushing winger, sending it out of play and winning a throw-in for his team

   c) welly it into the stands. You can't score from Row Z you know

2. Your team is a goal down with a minute to go. The ball is on the right side of midfield, but the opposition are defending in numbers and there are no free team-mates to pass to. Do you:

   a) run towards goal yourself, trying to go past any opposing players using a mixture of shimmies, lollipops and the occasional wall pass with a team-mate

   b) pass to one of the centre-backs, who can play the ball along the back line to the left wing, where there might be more space

   c) welly it up to the big man. You've got to stick it in the mixer in that kind of situation

3. Your name is Greg Shears. You are a diminutive striker. Your teammates know you as
   - [ ] a) Gregorinho
   - [ ] b) Greg
   - [ ] c) Shearsy

4. You love the World Cup, but you wish it didn't always have to end with
   - [ ] a) a hangover from some over-enthusiastic celebrations
   - [ ] b) a disappointing quarter-final defeat at the hands of an inferior nation, generally despite having held the lead for most of the game
   - [ ] c) a penalty shoot-out

5. You associate the word "banana" with the game of football because
   - [ ] a) of the "banana kicks" made famous by the great Rivelino in the 1970s, where the ball was sent round the wall before curling back towards goal with blatant disregard for the laws of physics
   - [ ] b) bananas are an excellent and rapidly-digested source of energy and extremely useful aids in terms of nutrition. They are also packed with iron, and are broken down rapidly by the body.
   - [ ] c) the FA Cup third round always forces a handful a Premiership teams to visit lowly opponents for fixtures they might lose. The technical term for these opponents is "potential banana skins".

6. Your chairman/president is
   - [ ] a) an idiot, remarkable only because his daughter is kidnapped annually
   - [ ] b) the most important person at the club, the country's former/current/future premier
   - [ ] c) a Russian billionaire

7. One day, you hope to wear
   - [ ] a) a World Cup winners' medal
   - [ ] b) an alice band and an enormous gold medallion
   - [ ] c) a page 3 girl on each arm, and a tattoo of your daughter's name in Sanskrit on your neck

8. When you were young, you always dreamed of playing for
   - [ ] a) your country
   - [ ] b) the pride of your family
   - [ ] c) lots of money

9. The most important skill in football is
   - [ ] a) the ability to use both feet with equal comfort
   - [ ] b) the discipline to obey the manager's instructions to the letter
   - [ ] c) the desire to win come what may and the heart to push yourself through the pain barrier if that's what it takes to bring home a victory for the boys

10. You met your wife in
    - [ ] a) the slums
    - [ ] b) mama's restaurant
    - [ ] c) Chinawhite

11. She looks like
    - [ ] a) a woman
    - [ ] b) the spitting image of you but with shorter hair and more make-up
    - [ ] c) a hairy pencil

12. The opposition's shirts are there to:
    - [ ] a) differentiate between you and your opponents
    - [ ] b) hang on to
    - [ ] c) be swapped at the end of the game and sent, via Fastframes, straight to your snooker room

13. As a centre-half, you feel
    - [ ] a) neglected and unloved, that you've lost life's lottery
    - [ ] b) you need coaching manuals when you've read Machiavelli
    - [ ] c) you are the manager's son

14. The person you'd most like to meet is:
    - [ ] a) The Pope
    - [ ] b) Clint Eastwood. You've already met The Pope
    - [ ] c) Snoop Doggy Dogg

15. To matches your fans bring:
    - [ ] a) a sense of rhythm and musical instruments
    - [ ] b) a sense of persecution, expensive sunglasses and impatience
    - [ ] c) a sense of divine right, eye-blistering lager breath and a few chants about the Second World War.

What the test tells us:

All A's: Latin America. Grant this man a work permit immediately. Watch out, however, for people who have generally answered A but say they're from Italy/Spain/Portugal. They almost certainly have a forged passport. Let them in anyway.

All B's: Southern Europe. Under European fair trade regulations this man must be allowed to enter the country

All C's: Great Britain. This man has no business presenting himself at an international border unless he has lost his passport. Return him to Football League HQ for processing. A large amount of confusion and an inability to answer any questions: This man may not yet be accurately reflected in this paper. Advise him to re-apply in six to twelve months. Yeah, we know we said it was a good system but nothing's perfect.

Cor. Wish I could get up that high...

FEBRUARY

Three days after moving to Liverpool, Robbie Fowler is fined £60 for speeding on his way to training. On the plus side, it's the easiest three points he's won for a while ... Sven-Goran Eriksson is ambushed by reporters in the Stockholm restaurant Den Vassa Eggen, where he says Guus Hiddink will get the England job − "and good luck to him" ... Mark Wright's January sacking by Peterborough was allegedly caused by him telling Sean St Ledger that he was "acting like a black man" ... Sol Campbell walks out of Highbury at half-time during Arsenal's 3−2 defeat by West Ham, with Sven watching. "He's very down. He's not well," says Arsène Wenger ... Joey Barton explains his decision to hand in a transfer request at Manchester City: "I never wanted to leave," he says, bizarrely ... Duncan Ferguson is fined two weeks' wages after being sent off for punching Wigan's Paul Scharner, bringing his career fines total over the £200,000 mark ... Graeme Souness is sacked by Newcastle ... The Littlewoods Cup, last won by Nottingham Forest in 1990 but which had gone missing, is found in a storeroom at the company's offices ... Two letters written by David Beckham when he was 16 are valued at £1,500 by auctioneers in Chester ... Tomasz Hajto, bought by Derby from Southampton during the transfer window, reveals that Clive Woodward once had to ask Nigel Quashie to explain the offside rule. "He knows nothing about football," says the defender ... Frank Lampard reveals that players make pre-match motivational speeches at Chelsea. "Me and John Terry do the majority of them," he says. "You talk about what comes into your head." In Terry's case, that'll be gambling and infidelity then. "Certain people shout and swear and certain people are more calm," Lamps says ... Alan Curbishley explains that Danny Murphy's move to Spurs was right for him, as he will "get invited to more film premieres than our players" ... Wayne Rooney takes Coleen to Eurodisney, where she is pictured riding Dumbo. Insert your own obvious punchline here ... "Fashion guru" Bruce Oldfield designs red uniforms for staff at the new Wembley ... Rooney is caught watching Chelsea play Liverpool in a pub at Eurodisney, where on the table in front of him sit a half-drunk pint of Fosters, a much-munched bowl of chips and the remains of some chicken wings ... Sol Campbell returns to Arsenal following a secret trip to Brussels. He says he's "feeling better" ... Middlesbrough lose 4−0 at home to Aston Villa. Their young defender Lee Cattermole cries at the final whistle. Villa's hat-trick hero Luke Moore promises to "give the ball to my mum". Mark Viduka gets in trouble after smiling and blowing a kiss to irate fans as he gets in his car, becoming after Stan Collymore only the second big-name striker to become known for romantic gestures in car parks ... Arjen Robben collapses to the ground clutching his throat to get Jose Reina sent off as Chelsea beat Liverpool ... In the African Nations Cup, Ivory Coast beat Cameroon 12–11 on penalties after a 1–1 draw. Samuel Eto'o is the only player to miss, after every single player had scored at the first attempt ... Roman Abramovich commissions a report into why Chelsea's fans aren't singing very much ... Gilberto says that when Sol Campbell returned from Brussels "everyone gave him a hug. It's like one big family at Arsenal" ... German police announce that anyone seen goose-stepping like Basil Fawlty will be arrested, as they unveil a new logo of a smiling cartoon officer that bears an uncanny resemblance to Adolf Hitler. "We're very disappointed," says a spokesman. "We cannot understand why somebody could think this smiling face is the dictator" ... Liverpool lose to Charlton, forcing Rafa Benitez into some extremely perceptive tactical analysis: "The problem is we are making too many mistakes" ... Spurs striker Mido is thrown out of Egypt's African Nations Cup squad after a blazing row with manager Hassan Shehata when he is substituted against Senegal. "You are nothing but a donkey," he shouts. "No, it is you who are the donkey," the manager replies. Mido's replacement scores the winner ... Everton's goalkeeper Richard Wright, who had previously injured his shoulder falling out of his parents' loft, trips over a sign telling him not to warm up in the Chelsea goalmouth and limps off clutching his leg. Iain Turner makes an unexpected debut and Everton lose 4–1 ... Workers at Wembley are pictured smoking cannabis ... David Moyes buys a £3.8m mansion with seven acres of land at Haighton Green, Preston ... Wayne Rooney announces that "of course we're going to win the World Cup". Franz Beckenbauer says that "to coach England is the best job in the world" ... Rio Ferdinand says: "I don't want to go another season without winning anything. Any trophy would do." The Manchester United squad hope to maximise their chances of silverware by entering Paul Scholes for Crufts. "He's our midfield terrier," one explains ... Victoria Beckham takes the children on a short skiing trip to the Pyrennes. Eschewing the traditional Alpine brands – Salomon, Berghaus, Peter Storm – she opts for £5,000 worth of Chanel for her two mornings on the nursery slopes ... Ron Atkinson is bitten by a venomous spider in the Caribbean and could have lost a leg but for the intervention of his wife who noticed his right peg was more swollen than usual ... The hunt is on for the identity of the gay footballer exposed by the *News of the World*. The soon to be late Peter Osgood does not wish to speculate on who the player might be but warns that he would not be happy to bathe alongside a homosexual team-mate ... Nicky Butt is left out of Birmingham's XVI for their evening game at Upton Park. He storms out of the team hotel and drives back to Birmingham, the most spritely act he's committed since leaving Old Trafford 18 months previously ... Portsmouth's new investor Sacha Gaydamak is "infuriated" that his £27m investment last month has so far yielded only one point ...

Managers of the month
FEBRUARY
Who won the awards:

PREMIERSHIP
Alan Pardew (West Ham)
Jim Hytner of the Barclays awards panel comments that Pardew has assembled a "talented crop" of young English players who "under his guidance will hopefully fulfil their ambitions with both club and country". Perhaps he thought he was giving the award to Steve McClaren. The man himself salutes "the best backroom staff in the country", another way of admitting that he's not that good.

CHAMPIONSHIP
Adrian Boothroyd (Watford)
"Not only has he had a great month, he has had a fantastic season," said former Hornets boss Graham Taylor, who is in no way biased towards all things Watford.

LEAGUE ONE
Martin Allen (Brentford)
Scooped the award despite not entirely convincing the panel of judges. "What a tight decision we had to make," said a less-than-usually enthusiastic Chris Kamara. "In the end we felt Martin just shaded it."

LEAGUE TWO
Keith Alexander (Lincoln City)
Just a single defeat in 17 league games – not all of them played in February – and four wins and a draw over the course of the month is award-winning form. "There's no such thing as an easy game at this stage of the season," he commented.

Who should have won the award:
Steve Evans (Boston)
It seems that derbies, even between Boston and Grimsby, can be heated affairs. Getting sent to the stands is nothing to boast about any more, but Evans went one better by being escorted from the dugout straight out of the ground and onto the team bus, where he followed the rest of the game on the radio. "Steve's no angel, and his language can be rather colourful at times," said his chairman Jon Sotnick, "but that in no way excuses how he was treated."

Fired!
High-profile casualties this month include former Arsenal ace Paul Merson, who promptly signs for Tamworth as a player. He didn't do much good there either, and had retired within a month. Also:

Keith Curle (Chester City)
Gary Megson (Nottingham Forest)
Martin Scott (Hartlepool)
Paul Merson (Walsall)
Graeme Souness (Newcastle United)

Hired!
Mark Wright (Chester City)
Paul Stephenson (Hartlepool United)
Kevan Broadhurst (Walsall)
Rob Kelly (Leicester City)

STATISTICS
Top scorers (league only):

Van Nistelrooy (Man Utd) – 19
Henry (Arsenal) – 15
Lampard (Chelsea) – 14

Yakubu (Middlesbrough) – 13
D Bent (Charlton) – 13

Top performers:

Most shots on target: **Lampard** (Chelsea) – 59
Most shots off target: **Rooney** (Man Utd) – 49
Most shots without scoring:
Jonathan Stead (Sunderland) – 39
Most offsides: **Darren Bent** (Charlton) – 46
Most free-kicks conceded:
Kevin Davies (Bolton) – 80

Match of the month
ARSENAL 2 WEST HAM UNITED 3

In which we learned a) Arsenal don't like it up 'em (though, on second thoughts, we probably knew that already). However, on this occasion they also don't like it round 'em or through 'em; b) Sol Campbell, having been blamed for two West Ham goals, "was very down at half-time". This according to Arsène Wenger, who was appraised of the fact during a tete-a-tete in the Highbury toilets. The giant centre-back reacted to his poor state of mind by leaving the ground and fleeing to Belgium. He didn't play again until April. So the other players weren't so down at half-time? Were they cheerful? We demand answers; c) The perfect way to bury bad news is to create some worse news. The mysterious disappearance of a large England international made everyone forget all about West Ham, who played very well; d) Wenger, always diplomatic, later announced that "Sol has shown a weakness in his life". West Ham, meanwhile, showed a weakness in his team. Once February was over, however, they didn't lose again in the league.

Top of the table

		P	W	D	L	F	A	GD	Pts
1	CHELSEA	27	22	3	2	54	16	38	69
2	MANCHESTER UNITED	26	16	6	4	52	27	25	54
3	LIVERPOOL	27	16	6	5	33	17	16	54
4	SPURS	27	12	10	5	37	24	13	46
5	BLACKBURN ROVERS	27	13	4	10	34	31	3	43

Bottom of the table

		P	W	D	L	F	A	GD	Pts
16	MIDDLESBROUGH	26	8	7	11	35	44	-9	31
17	WEST BROM	27	7	5	15	24	40	-16	26
18	BIRMINGHAM CITY	26	6	5	15	22	37	-15	23
19	PORTSMOUTH	27	4	6	17	18	47	-29	18
20	SUNDERLAND	27	2	4	21	18	49	-31	10

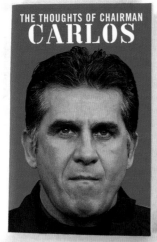

THE THOUGHTS OF CHAIRMAN
CARLOS

CARLOS QUEIROZ'S
FOOTBALL HANDBOOK
MODULE 7 – OUT OF THE OVEN, INTO THE BAKERY

"**I WAS LOOKING** at my lower division tables and I couldn't help but notice that Reading have practically wrapped up the Championship title already. I heard one commentator say that they are "on a roll". This is a problem that they will need to have conquered before they kick off in the Premiership, because you will get absolutely nowhere while balanced on baked goods. You can get away with that kind of behaviour in the lower leagues, but not at this level. Imagine the state they will be in, trying to keep up with top-flight teams like that! No, baked goods must be left outside the Madejski Stadium altogether otherwise they'll be cream slicing their shots all over the place and they'll have muffin to show for their promotion other than a donut-sized hole in their midfield. They're going to have to rise when the temperature is at its highest. Do I make myself clear?"

Theo's Diary

My new school's rubbish. I remember one of Mum's friends back home saying how in London nobody speaks English in schools and it's true. Everyone's from abroad and they're all like 30 and married and don't like to play Top Trumps with me on the coach. I played my first game for the school team in the reserves, which is exactly the same as the normal team except with nobody watching.

Gordon Strachan's cheeseboard
Yarg

ALL RIGHT, IT SOUNDS LIKE what someone says when they're tackled by Roy Keane but this fella certainly doesn't take a kicking in the taste department. It's a bit prickly, though it's doesn't always have the maturity that I look for in my cheeses. Like even the best signings, it changes its style as it gets older, and in the end becomes a bit crumbly. It can be hard to tell when it's at the perfect stage for eating. Watch out, though, because the price rises as it gets older but if you your cheese is too aged it'll just fall apart and be next to useless. At that stage, you might want to substitute it for something that offers a bit more cream.

Welcome to... Liverpool

Fernando Morientes certainly made himself comfortable after signing from Real Madrid. So comfortable was he, in fact, that within weeks of his high-profile arrival he was displaying his exaggerated levels of comfort on the bench, rather than being forced to do nasty strenuous stuff that he wasn't that good at anyway. But still life was not as good as it seemed, and secretly he yearned to return home. Actually not that secretly, because he told a journalist about it. "Arriving from Madrid made Liverpool look like an ugly city, especially because of the rotten weather, which makes the city look sad." So far, so book-me-on-the-next-flight-out-of-this-hellhole, but all was not lost as he added, somewhat sheepishly: "But I've completely fallen under the spell of the club." Sadly for the Scousers the spell appeared to have sent him to sleep.

(Continued from p.75)

Romance

5. Model shoots

A few steps beyond the beauty contest. Thierry Henry is the most famous exponent of this art, having met his wife Nicole Merry on the set of a Renault Clio advert in 2001. The less imaginative can always keep an eye on *The Sun's* Page 3, a regular production line for FWs (see Rio Ferdinand and Holly McGuire) though buxom beauty Nicola T denied that her relationship with Bobby Zamora was in any way stereotypical. "I love Bobby because he's Bobby, not because he's a footballer," she said.

6. Other footballers

If you're stuck, you can always ask a team-mate for the number of one of their exes. Cristiano Ronaldo has gone out with Lauren Frain, former belle of another Manchester United star, Alan Smith. Some FWs have engaged in serial relationships with footballers. Take, for example, Leilani, who was married to former Wimbledon and Watford "ace" Mark Williams and also dated Kieron Dyer before getting engaged to French forward Jeremie Aliadiere.

7. Out shopping

The award for vigilance at all times goes to Aberdeen's Darren Mackie, who once spotted a pretty girl called Jenni shopping with her mum in the Inverurie branch of Tesco. They are now married.

DATING

So you've met a girl. That's the first stage. Maybe she's given you her number. You might even have exchanged a few saucy text messages (Jermaine Jenas is apparently a master of this particular art). Now you've got to arrange a meeting. Asking a girl out on a date is always a nervous occasion, and even the finest footballers can fear rejection. Perhaps that's why Cristiano Ronaldo asked his interpreter to call one of his former conquests, nurse-turned-model Julie Hawkins. Many women would be unimpressed, but the Portuguese winger's poor English didn't stop Hawkins from saying yes – and not just to a meal out. "As he undressed me he looked at my thighs and gasped: 'You, footballer' when he saw how toned they were. When I mimed riding a horse to show him how I got them that way it seemed to excite him all the more. The only words Cristiano managed to utter while we were romping were 'Hot, Julie, hot', which made me burst into fits of laughter."

Not every woman says yes, and sometimes you need persistence. Alex Curran said no the first time Steven Gerrard called, and Cheryl Tweedy didn't initially melt to Ashley Cole's charms. "I saw him playing tennis and he'd look at me like he fancied me," she recounts. "I'd tut and look away. One day he asked for my number and I said no in front of all of his friends." She only changed her mind when a psychic told her that her spirits were hinting at a relationship with a fooballer. Well, with evidence like that you would, wouldn't you?

In Curran's case, her friends convinced her she was making a mistake and eventually she said yes. That only led to the second problem: the first date. Rooney took Coleen to their local chip shop on their first date, but not everyone can afford such an exclusive location – Gerrard and Curran spent their first evening together babysitting her brother. "I was so embarrassed," she said. "We just sat there." Their next attempt was only slightly better. "We went for a meal and a few drinks, then danced all night," she said. "Steven fell asleep in the taxi and the driver couldn't wake him up."

But not every first date leads to a second. Alex Williams of Scottish club Clyde recalls that he once arranged a date with a girl he had met in a nightclub. The problem was, he had forgotten what she looked like. "When I saw her I just told the taxi driver to keep going," he said. "She was straight on the phone, calling me an arsehole!"

On the subject of poor behaviour during dates, may we introduce you to "curvy" Alisha Jarratt, former squeeze of England left-back Wayne Bridge, and her tale of woe from one meeting with the player. "He was still sweaty from playing," she said. "With every piece of clothing he took off the pong just got worse. I did suggest he had a shower but he was so eager we just got down to it." Their relationship, inevitably, didn't last. "Wayne only loves himself," she added. (Cont. p.124)

Balls

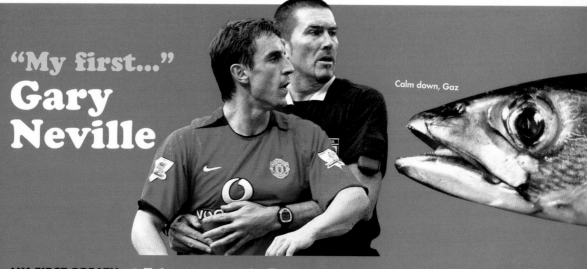

Calm down, Gaz

"My first..."
Gary Neville

MY FIRST BREATH 18 February 1975 in Bury, so that means I'm now ... er ... give me a minute ... I'll get this ... um ... come back to me.

MY FIRST CLUB Manchester United, who I signed for as a schoolboy in 1991.

MY FIRST BIG SPORTING ACHIEVEMENT I scored a century in the Bolton cricket league in 1992. Probably not what United had in mind when they signed me, but there you go.

MY FIRST OPPORTUNITY TO MENTION MY FATHER'S FUNNY NAME He's called Neville Neville, as everyone knows. Everyone also knows that my sister Tracey played netball for England.

MY FIRST STRIKE I haven't actually gone on one yet, though I've tried really, really hard. I work dead hard for the players' union because even though we earn loads of money we've still got rights.

MY FIRST STRIKE BALLOT After Rio Ferdinand was dropped by England when he missed a drug test. Which is his right, obviously.

MY FIRST SLIGHTLY STRANGE JOB I became tourism ambassador for Malta in 2001. It's a really nice place, honest. You should go there.

MY FIRST REVELATION THAT I HATE SCOUSERS I never said that. I never said: "I hate Scousers'," I said once, "I grew up not liking Liverpool because they won everything." So that sets the record straight, eh? No hard feelings, like.

MY FIRST BIG FAT LIE What I said about not hating Scousers. Because a couple of years later I said: "I can't stand Liverpool, I can't stand Liverpool people, I can't stand anything to do with them." Though my kid brother Phil's a Scouser now, which is a problem.

MY FIRST BIG COMPLIMENT I'd won England caps and stuff but I was really happy at what the gaffer Sir Alex Ferguson said about me in February 2006. "I'd rather have Gary Neville in my team than some kind of cold fish," he said. I was really chuffed, like. Though come to think of it, I haven't got a clue what he meant.

THE HARD SELL

OR: CLAUDE MAKELELE TAKES SOME TIME OFF

Claude Makelele reveals he went on a trip to Lourdes "to find some spiritual calm". "I was able to spend time at such a sacred place and talk with the monks about my faith," he reports.

SCENE: Makelele and the 'Special One' are talking...

Makelele: Hey, gaffer. The big man. Special one. How's it hanging?

Mourinho: Er, Claude you seem to be behaving very strangely.

Makelele: What makes you say that?

Mourinho: Well, you haven't been booked for two months for a start. It seems you are not attacking the opponents with your usual aggression.

Makelele: It is true. To be honest, I need to pay homage.

Mourinho: Well really Claude, there's no need to be like that.

Makelele: No really gaffer, I need to be inspired, to rediscover my spiritual strength by basking in the healing waters …

Mourinho: You know very well that my bathroom is strictly off limits.

Makelele: … and speaking with people who can fill me with passion and surprise me with their faith.

Mourinho: Well if you insist, I might be free for dinner on Sunday.

Makelele: No gaffer, I am speaking about Lourdes!

Mourinho: Madonna's awkwardly-named first child?

Makelele: No, Lourdes!

Mourinho: The spiritual home of cricket?

Makelele: No, the French spring town. I must go there and see Our Lady of Lourdes.

Mourinho: I'm not giving you time off to visit some French floozy. I've read about you in the papers, I know what you're like.

Makelele: Believe me, this is important. It is a place where injuries are healed, where broken souls are put back together. I'm serious. It's a pilgrimage.

Mourinho: A pilgrimage? Well, I guess so. But you'd better not be going there on foot, you'll do your hamstring.

TOP 10
FOOTBALLING PETS

1 / IVAN CAMPO

Bolton Wonderers midfielder Ivan Campo has a pet dog. In August 2005 the pampered pooch pooed on Beesley Green in Worsley and when he failed to scoop it up he earned a £50 fine (which he failed to pay). A Worsley council spokesman stood up for the Spaniard, insisting "it was simply to do with the language barrier and the footballer not knowing how the system works". Which is nonsense – Campo could write a book about fouling, although unlike his pavement-spoiling hound most of his misdemeanours take place on grass. Still, it brings a whole new meaning to the term "relegation dog-fight".

2 / PAUL JEWELL

One of football's great left-wingers (sadly not on the pitch), Jewell has a habit of naming his pets after great socialist figures. That's why he called his tortoise Trotsky.

3 / DANNY MURPHY'S MENAGERIE

Danny Murphy and his wife Joanna Taylor have two Bernese mountain dogs and a Labrador, and adopted a stray they found on holiday in India. Charlton's run of good form at the start of last season coincided with the arrival of the second mountain dog, which his wife was house-training at the time. As soon as it learned to do its business outside, Murphy himself forgot. "We both love dogs," Taylor said in August 2005. "They're good to have around because it is nice to have something to divert your attention [from the start of the new season]. The build-up to the new season is always exciting. I've been drinking a lot more as a result." The last bit of that quote is not strictly relevant here, but it saves us from having to do a "Footballers' Alcoholic Partners" chapter.

4 / ANDY GRAY

Has two dogs – Rocky and Teddy. Last year he gave an interview to K9 Magazine (no really, he did) in which they were described as "grape-munching mutts".

5 / JAMIE REDKNAPP

Has two bulldogs, Winston and Bella. His wife Louise takes them for a walk every day. "This gets rid of about 240 calories an hour," one interview with the former popstrel pointed out, helpfully.

6/BRIAN JENSEN

The Burnley goalkeeper is called The Beast and aptly enough he owns a nine-and-a-half stone rottweiler called Timmy. When the Dutchman and his dog were emotionally reunited after its quarantine (the dog's, that is), the Airport TV cameras were there to capture the scene. "Big as he is, he's so friendly," gushed the goalie. "There's a golden retriever in a rottweiler costume."

7/DARREN BARNARD

The then Barnsley star suffered the best pet-based injury ever in 1998 when he slipped on the kitchen lino after his pet dog peed on the floor. The torn ligaments kept him out of the game for five months. "It was my first major injury," he said. "It kept me out months, but what made it worse was a freak accident in my kitchen when I slipped on my puppy Zak's dog muck. That set me back weeks."

8/ENRIQUE ROMERO

In 2004 the Spanish full-back had a notable animal-related injury double-whammy. The first was one of those everyday things that must make the physio at any football club roll his eyes, so common is it: he was bitten while attempting to charm a snake at Pamplona airport. Like you do. Then there was a nasty cycling accident caused when Romero swerved to avoid a friend's pet dog when it ran into his path and fell awkwardly. "He has serious bruising to his right buttock," explained the Deportivo La Coruna club doctor. "It's the kind of accident that could happen to anyone." Another canine-related injury cost French defender Julien Escude a move to Manchester United in 2002, when he tripped over while walking his dog and twisted his left knee.

9/WAYNE ROONEY

Who earns a place in the list for buying Coleen McLoughlin an elephant, even though it was only through an adopt-an-African-animal scheme and cost £20 so doesn't really count. He later bought her a horse though.

10/MATT OAKLEY

They say pets resemble their owners and Oakley's animal collection is like the man himself – quite boring on the face of it, but with unexpected bite below the surface. The midfielder has a black Labrador called Donald (dull) and a tank full of piranhas (better). "I think the normal sort of fish you put in tanks, such as angel fish, tetras and guppies, are a bit boring," he says. "I just have to be careful of my fingers!" Talented – and funny as well. "They are evil-looking things," his former team-mate James Beattie said. "He feeds them on mincemeat but they prefer live earthworms."

MARCH

John Toshack gets his excuses in early before Wales take on Paraguay: "I got everything wrong in Cyprus and it rubbed off on the players – but if you see another performance like that it won't be my fault". It'll be Robbie Savage's ... Barcelona supremo Joan Laporta accuses Chelsea of "dirty tricks" in the run up to their Champions League decider ... Robbie Williams invests £250,000 in Port Vale. Hopefully "No Regrets". More likely "Something Stupid" ... Real Zaragoza fined £6,120 for racist chants aimed at Barcelona's Samuel Eto'o ... Romanian outfit Regal Hornia sign UT Arad defender Marius Cioara for a fee of 15 kilograms of sausages. Mark Viduka contacts his agent ... The Lord of the Manor of Frodsham signs up for car makeover show *Pimp My Ride* with the son of the former Bishop of Rochester Tim Westwood. The crazily coiffed, soon-to-be-jettisoned Djibril reveals his Chrysler is already adorned with a portrait of the face of his four-year-old daughter on the bonnet. The landed gentry, eh? No longer a case of U and non U, more like I and Fuck U ... A specially designed England shirt for dogs goes on sale at £4.99 ... Peter Osgood dies aged 59 ... England beat Uruguay 2-1 thanks to a late winner from Joe Cole ... the two substitutes, Shaun Wright Phillips at 5ft 6in and Peter Crouch at 6ft 7in wait to be brought on standing side-by-side. ... Sven pleads with England fans to stop singing the "Ten German bombers" song. It's back to the IRA, then ... Sir Alex Ferguson admits he falls in love with his players. "It's hard to say goodbye," he explains. So that's why he prefers "Piss off, you're sold" instead ... David Beckham tells a Spanish magazine "something supernatural guides me, judges me". That was Sir Alex, but you're free now ... Jermaine "positively the final, final, final chance" Pennant is kicked out of The Works nightclub in Birmingham at the end of the Kanye West after show party ... Jeff Winter signs copies of his autobiography at Middlesbrough's club shop. Two people turn up ... Steve Bruce tells Jermaine "this is seriously your ultimate last chance, stop sniggering" Pennant to grow up. "If he leads his life properly the world is his oyster" ... Big Sam says England are missing out on a modern day David Platt by not picking Kevin "Captain Birdseye" Nolan ... David O'Leary tells Aston Villa fans to "get real" and stop living in the past ... Lee Hendrie admits common assault after an incident at a Solihull taxi rank. He's sentenced to 60 hours community service ... A Japanese fan offers £1,000 at auction for a robe worn by David Beckham … Sunderland's Tommy Miller tells the fans "it could be worse". How, exactly? … Former Leicester boss Peter Taylor admits he deserves to be booed by Leicester fans. "if I'd have been a Leicester fan I'd have been disappointed." … Rio the parrot, named after the England defender, pledges his support for the national team after learning a string of chants. "He's as smart as half our World Cup side,' boasts his owner Gary Prickler … Glen Johnson misses Chelsea's flight to Barcelona after forgetting his passport … Chelsea are knocked out, but undeservedly so, says Jose Mourinho, who is then described in a Catalan newspaper as the "translator of shit" … Brad Friedel announces he wants to play "until I drop". Sign for Birmingham, son and you'll drop like a stone … Ruud van Nistelrooy is again left out of Manchester United XI for the match against Wigan and is, according to a "friend", "peed off". So is Underground Ernie Lineker, reprimanded by the BBC for his pre-historic "why the long face Ruud?" gag … Craig Bellamy is arrested after an alleged altercation with a 19-year-old female in Cardiff nightclub Number 10 … It emerges that Glen Johnson was spotted partying hours before he was due to fly out to Barcelona … An Arsenal side containing no English players beat Real Madrid … Ronald Koeman labels Liverpool "easy meat" after his Benfica side knock out the Reds … Robbie Savage claims Welsh assistant manager Roy Evans wants him back in the side but will "wait my time for Toshack to go because I'm confident he'll be found out" … Johan Cruyff calls Jose Mourinho "a learner" … Falkirk and Trinidad striker Russell Latapy admits smoking 40 fags a day. Well if was good enough for Socrates … Alpay rejects the offer of an anger management course from his club Cologne after being given a six-game ban by the Turkish FA … Alan Pardew claims that Arsenal's foreign player policy is jeopardising "the soul of English football". Instead of pointing to the hypocrisy of a man who is prepared to sanction holiday apartheid for his players by sending his two Israeli citizens to Spain on their own while taking the rest of the squad to Dubai, Arsène Wenger calls Pardew a racist. Pardew is upset … Barnet defender Ian Hendon joins the bizarre injury XI after gashing his left toe when trying to stop a plate smashing on the floor while cooking … Ian Wright set to put overweight teenagers through their paces in new Channel 4 show "Fitter Kids". He went from being the king of Highbury to Mr Saturday night. Now he's the new Green Goddess … Posh and Becks agree an out of court settlement with the *News of the World* over accusations that their marriage was on the rocks … Alan Hansen, Ian Wright and Jamie Redknapp front the new Marks and Spencer Autograph range. It's decent at the back, good up front but the middle needs holding together by its dad … David Dunn releases the pressure before Birmingham's relegation six- pointer with West Brom by announcing he'll "always have a big arse" … A Spanish policewoman wins damages from a TV station which accused her of eyeing up David Beckham. A commentator joked that she was giving the England skipper "a good going over" … Harry Redknapp says that striker Benjani is struggling in front of goal because he's so shy … A professional David Beckham lookalike is also discovered to be "on the game", offering certain services for £500 a night. Yes, there's sex, but he'll also line up all your towels and make sure the cans in your fridge all face the same way…

Managers of the month

MARCH

Who won the awards:

PREMIERSHIP

Sir Alex Ferguson
(Manchester United)
Out of Europe and the FA Cup, it was time to concentrate on the league and Ferguson's team racked up five wins to cut Chelsea's lead to seven points. An analysis of those successive victories – Wigan, Newcastle, Birmingham, West Brom and West Ham – would suggest that Ferguson would have expected to win them whether a magnum of Barclays bubbly was at stake or not.

CHAMPIONSHIP

Rob Kelly (Leicester City)
Three wins and a draw is award-winning form – even if no-one really knows who you are.

LEAGUE ONE

Frank Barlow & Ian McParland
(Nottingham Forest)
Chris will be giving the award to Hong Kong Phooey next month if he's not careful as again it's gone to a caretaker, or to be precise, a pair of caretakers. And dual managers have such a great track record: Stevens and McLeary? One quickly sacked. Curbishley and Gritt. One quickly sacked. Houllier and Evans ... you get the picture.

LEAGUE TWO

Paul Simpson (Carlisle United)
Carlisle, according to Chris, "have been nothing short of sensational" and their tally of 16 goals in five games and position at the top of the table makes us want to agree. But we won't because "nothing short of sensational" sounds like something Tony Blackburn would say when introducing a knife-thrower's scarred but still game "lovely assistant, Sandra." And that can't be right.

Who should have won the award:
Glenn Roeder (Newcastle United)
One win and three defeats in March does not look that impressive but hey, this is Newcastle we're talking about and we're starting from a pretty low base. He got Wor Alan to the magic figure, he looks good in serious spectacles, there is no finer lip-purser in top-flight football and he got Shola Ameobi occasionally to lift his head.

Fired!
A relatively calm month, during which chairmen generally decide to give their struggling managers a couple more games to prove they can turn things round. Then, come April, they sack 'em.
Brian Talbot (Oxford United)
Mick McCarthy (Sunderland)

Hired!
Jim Smith (Oxford United)

STATISTICS

Top scorers (league only):

Van Nistelrooy (Man Utd) – 20
Henry (Arsenal) – 19
D Bent (Charlton) – 16
Lampard (Chelsea) – 14
Harewood (West Ham) – 14

Top performers:

Most shots on target: **Rooney** (Man Utd) – 61
Most shots off target: **Rooney** (Man Utd) – 65
Most shots without scoring:
Stead (Sunderland) – 40
Most offsides: **Bent** (Charlton) – 57
Most free-kicks won: **Boa Morte** (Fulham) – 93

Match of the month
FULHAM 1 CHELSEA 0

In which we discovered: 1) If you put an Easter Island statue on castors and got Betty Turpin from Coronation Street to push it up a hill, it would be more mobile than Robert Huth. 2) Systems, at least the ones used by Jose Mourinho, are never wrong; it's only ever poor execution of revolutionary tactics by the players that causes problems. And if you have to substitute two players habitually low on confidence, say Shaun Wright-Phillips and Joe Cole, after 26 minutes of the match to emphasise this point and deflect attention from your own mistakes, then so be it. 3) That Andy Gray hates referees is hardly news but his odd logic over Didier Drogba's "equaliser" takes the Rich Tea. Drogba blatantly hand-balled, the decision made is correct in every respect except for Gray's assertion that the linesman and referee shouldn't have made it because they weren't in a position to see the offence properly. Hammer a player for cheating? Never. Slam a referee for getting something right? Why not?

Top of the table		P	W	D	L	F	A	GD	Pts
1	CHELSEA	31	25	3	3	60	19	41	78
2	MANCHESTER UNITED	31	21	6	4	62	29	33	69
3	LIVERPOOL	32	19	7	6	45	22	23	64
4	TOTTENHAM HOTSPUR	31	15	10	6	45	29	16	55
5	BLACKBURN ROVERS	31	16	4	11	42	36	6	52
Bottom of the table									
16	ASTON VILLA	31	8	11	12	34	41	-7	35
17	WEST BROM	31	7	6	18	28	47	-19	27
18	BIRMINGHAM CITY	30	6	6	18	23	44	-21	24
19	PORTSMOUTH	30	6	6	18	24	51	-27	24
20	SUNDERLAND	31	2	4	25	19	55	-36	10

CARLOS QUEIROZ'S

FOOTBALL HANDBOOK

MODULE 8

" PEOPLE ASK ME if I am jealous of Arsenal and their Champions League progress. Of course not, because I would like to think I have played my part. You see when they went through that season unbeaten a couple of years ago, they played too flashy. Now they string five across the midfield, soak up pressure and rely on one striker to kill people on the counter attack. This is proper, sophisticated football, strictly for the connoisseur. It's something I have had in mind for a long time. In fact it is vindication of my teaching. We used to play with two bombers in the centre of midfield and two wingers crossing for twin strikers. And we last won the league in 2003 playing like that. But we'd never win in Europe playing like that so we switched to all out attack by going to one upfront. Now I see that we needed someone as quick as Thierry Henry to make it work properly. Our Dutch penalty-box lurker just doesn't fit the bill but we signed a pigeon-catcher to be our Henry and I have never seen anyone with such pace. Yes, David Bellion is coming along very nicely and will soon be ready to take centre stage. We've sold him you say? Oh ... I've always said Dutch centre-forwards who score 20 goals a season are invaluable if you play to their strengths. If ... "

Theo's Diary

My French teacher has been trying to teach me foreign languages, but none of them are French. This month he took me to Madrid and to Turin, which is in Italy. I'd never been on an exchange before and it was lots of fun and I think they must have really liked us because both times we played a special game of football just before we came home and at the end of it my team was really happy but they were very very sad.

Stuart Pearce's cheeseboard
Kraft Singles & Dairylea

I WANT CHEESE THAT'LL DO A JOB and for that you don't want airy fairy foreign muck. They're British, and British is best God bless Her Majesty; they're cheap, and cheap is good, and, having once been massive they've learned to live in the shadow of the ultimate big cheese. But they're as honest as the day is long. I can't fault them for that. And they put the effort in too. No word of a lie. A bit middle of the road? Promise more than they actually deliver? No way. When I was in the 100 Club watching Subway Sect, was triangular cheese seen as bland then? If it was good enough for the greats then it's good enough for an humble cheesemonger still with his L-plates stuck on, do you mind if I self-deprecate further and just tug this forelock, you've got a very difficult job and I appreciate you being so kind to me, give us your shoes I'll give them a quick wipe …

Welcome to...
Valencia

Pass us the ketchup, mate, I hate this fishy crap

On the face of it Levante left-back Ian Harte did well to flee Yorkshire and make a new home for himself in the birthplace of paella, but he wasn't sitting on his laurels. "It has been very difficult for me in Spain right from the start," he said, sounding very much like every British export ever. "I don't like to be here. Valencia is a nice city but it was better living in England. I don't have friends here. When training finishes I just go back to the house and that's basically it."
Bet it's a brilliant house, though.

HARRY REDKNAPP'S
Dossier
✦ ✦ ✦ ✦ ✦ ✦ ✦ March 2006 ✦ ✦ ✦ ✦ ✦ ✦ ✦

'Arry's book — KEEP OUT

Portsmouth F.C.

Southampton F.C

PORTSMOUTH F.C.

Effing hard work, this management business, I can tell you. It's not easy coming up with an endless list of transfer targets when some Russian geezer turns up with a fancy car and a big cheque book. It's even harder contriving somehow to lose loads of games even with a newly revamped squad, though it does give you chance to get on telly and try out a few self-deprecating jokes. It's always good to put people down, and it doesn't matter if it's yourself.

But it all turned round this month after Pedro Mendes smacked in a couple of stupid goals against Man City to get the boys all fired up. They might not have known each other's names but if they would struggle to order each other around on the pitch they didn't struggle when it came to ordering each other a round at the bar, I can tell you. Excellent team spirit we've got here, excellent.

The other day in training I turned to young Andres d'Alessandro, Argentinian chap we've got in on loan, one of the great midfielders in Europe if you ask me, and I said: "Oi Andres, hop it over there and send in some long ones for Benny to get on the end of son, there's a good fella." He looked at me as if I was flippin' mental. Didn't understand a word he didn't. Effing hard work, this.

We had to put in some extra practice because we was off back to Upton Park, always an 'ard place to go and all the more so if you've got some History. The fans was on me back from the moment I walked in there but that was as hard as it got because they played a joke team against us, something about a cup game, and we won again. Still, you can only beat what's put in front of you, ain't it. People talking about a miracle escape already, it doesn't half put the wind up you that kind of talk. Long way off that is.

Hang on a minute, I've just realised this is a private dossier, for your eyes only, never to be read by the general public. Does that mean I can stop using that ludicrous cockney accent? Well, thank heavens for that! I've had it up to here with all that faux-east-end nonsense. Matron always said that it was worth being able to communicate with the commoners but I didn't know back at boarding school that I'd have to do this much of it. I'm still not sure I've got it down pat, to tell the truth. I think I tend to throw in a few too many colloquialisms. I had myself down for a career in the diplomatic corps, frankly. I thought I'd follow my father into the colonies, and for more than just deciding whether I should sign Benjamin Mwaruwari. Still, I've had a lovely career and a spiffing few months, I'd say, and if we stay up it would be splendid. The commentators will be calling me a genius and regaling me with silverware, but they just don't get it at all. It's nothing to do with me whatsoever. You see, it's not just Andres d'Alessandro who can't understand what I'm saying – it's the whole bleeding lot of them.

Balls

Fernando Morientes
Liverpool

Ay caramba! I was thees close...

Born: 5 April 1976.
Signed: for £6.3m from Real Madrid: January 2005.
Sold: to Valencia for £3.1m in May 2006.
Career totals: 454 games, 169 goals, 0.37 goals per game
Liverpool totals: 60 games, 12 goals, 0.2 goals per game
Interesting fact: His father, brother and uncle are all policemen
Marks out of 10: International Reputation 9; Long History Of Goal-scoring Prowess 9; Sudden Loss Of Form 9; Sense Of Excitement When He Signed 9; Sense Of Disappointment When He Left 2

A career in quotes

Morientes says: "When you leave Madrid you need to go to another club that fills you with hope and enthusiasm and Liverpool does that for me."

Rafael Benitez says: "We have signed a very important player for this club, for the team and the supporters. He is very crucial to us in terms of the confidence he can bring to the side."

Morientes boasts: "I think I will adapt quickly. I will have to get used to the physical side of the game and more contact."

Steven Gerrard notes: "It's only a matter of time before he clicks. You can see just by some of the little things he does how good he is. I think the fans will really love him."

Morientes says: "I am not affected by criticism. If I can drive out after training or out of Anfield after a game and tell myself I've done the very best I can, I am happy."

Florentino Perez says: "All the girls love him – more than they do David Beckham."

Benitez says: "We know he can play better, he knows he can play better, and he wants to play better. Fernando will improve, I'm sure."

Morientes notes, 12 May: "I would like to finish my career here at Liverpool. I had 14 happy years in Spain but I don't ever plan to go back as a footballer."

Morientes concludes, 26 May: "Valencia is a great club and for any professional it's a great opportunity to play here."

THE HARD SELL

SCENE: Brian Barwick and Big Phil Scolari are having a bit of a chin wag about a job that's coming up...

Brian Barwick:

"As you know we've got a vacancy to fill and we think you might be the man to fill it."

Luis 'Big Phil' Felipe Scolari:

"How gratifying, tell me more."

Barwick: "Well it's the highest-paid job in international football. You get to manage the team from the game's birthplace with millions of fans so passionate they customise their vehicles like May parade floats during tournaments. You'll get to mould Wayne Rooney, the flower of a golden generation of talent, shape the destiny of young prospects as good as Theo Walcott and Aaron Lennon, you'll get to converse with the finest minds in the game – Mourinho, Ferguson, Wenger, Bassett – you will become the head of the home of football, go anywhere, see anything, play about eight games on average a year and live in Europe's most bustling capital city."

Scolari: "Highest-paid job in international football, you say?"

Barwick: "Yes, but we've had our fingers burnt before. Tell me have you done or said anything the press won't like? What would you do if a man dressed in white robes came up to you and said: 'Ere guv, er sorry effendi, how do you fancy managing the Villa'? Do you have serial pant-dropping tendencies? Can you handle the pressure of a defeat and not throw in the towel minutes after a game? Any thoughts on the disabled? Disqualified as a director? Name easily transposed with that of a root vegetable?"

Scolari: "None of these things. I have led an exemplary life with no skeletons in my closet at all. I have put it on record that I'm not overly fond of having gays in my team and while I admit General Pinochet tortured a lot of people I also point out that there is no illiteracy in Chile. See there is balance in everything I say.

Barwick: "Jesus! But you'd still be interested. I need to report back to the boss, er, Mr Dein."

Scolari: "Yes, in principle, as long as the press leave me alone. You can guarantee that can't you? Why are you weeping? Are you leaving already? You'll be in touch, you say?"

Nightclubs

Continued from p.89

UMBABA, LONDON

15-21 Ganton Street, W1 / Tel. 020 7734 6696
www.umbaba.com

It can be difficult finding a new spin for old interiors. The problem is, most good ideas have already been done. Anyway, come here for a décor "inspired by a pastiche of African Culture through the ages from the Butabu style of Western Africa through to colonial safari and shanty town chic". Further comment is unnecessary.

Tabloid tales

Joe Cole was seen last December "looking cold" as he left the club (it actually was cold, so it's not entirely surprising), while Jimmy Floyd Hasselbaink was seen with a "brunette friend" who he "abandoned" every time a photographer appeared. Cheryl Tweedy had her hen night here in July, drinking £220 bottles of pink champagne with her Girls Aloud chums.

KABARETS PROPHECY, LONDON

16-18 Beal Street, W1 (though the entrance is in Upper John Street, confusingly) / Tel. 020 7439 2229
www.kabaretsprophecy.com

With a capacity of just 100 it's only slightly bigger than our living room but nevertheless bills itself as "the ultimate, luxury play den".

Tabloid tales

Not strictly speaking linked to footballers, but this is where England's Ashes-winning team chose to celebrate their success so it must have something going for it. Probably not the prices, though – their night here cost them £25,000.

TOAST, HAMPSTEAD, LONDON

50 Hampstead High Street, NW3 1QG
Tel. 020 7431 2244 / www.toastnw3.com

The reigning best bar in Hampstead is an unusual celebrity hang-out, but the food's nice, apparently.

Tabloid tales

Rio Ferdinand and Jody Morris got angry when accosted by a photographer outside the bar. The argument apparently ended with the cameraman on the ground and Ferdinand, having thrown some CDs at the mean man, encouraging his friend to "kill him, stamp on his head". A "diner" said he told the England defender to "leave it, you've got the World Cup coming up".

FACES, ILFORD, ESSEX

458 Cranbrook Road IG2
www.facesnightclub.co.uk

"Generally regarded as the coolest club around" – by the owners themselves no less.

Tabloid Tales

Where John Terry first met Lianne Johnson (see Brown's, above). "He was with that Kevin Adams from Fame Academy and some other friends," she said. "He didn't buy me any drinks because I was already drunk."

Continued p.127

Is anything worse than Chelsea?

Football is all about action. It is what people do that counts. But sometimes what they say can be even more revealing. Didier Drogba: "Sometimes I dive, sometimes I stay up. But I don't care about this. In football, you can't stay up every time." Chelsea FC became villains of the month after Shaun Wright-Phillips fell over Newcastle's Robbie Elliott to get the defender sent off and Drogba, in between theatrical tumbles, controlled with his hand to score both against Fulham (disallowed) and Manchester City (not).

Balls! **set out to see where Chelsea stand on the list of hated things.**

1. Brussels Sprouts
❑ Better than Chelsea: because they actually improve your blood pressure
❑ Just as bad as Chelsea: at leaving a bad taste in the mouth
❑ Worse than Chelsea: because they don't go down easily
Verdict: Chelsea are worse

2. Celebrity Love Island
❑ Better than Chelsea: because at the end of the season they go away and don't come back
❑ Just as bad as Chelsea: paying their stars too much money to do very little
❑ Worse than Chelsea: because they actively encourage their stars to fall head over heels, even if they rarely succeed
Verdict: Chelsea are worse

3. Traffic wardens
❑ Better than Chelsea: you at least get the right to appeal
❑ Just as bad as Chelsea: they hit you with penalties you don't think you deserve — and seem to get pleasure from it
❑ Worse than Chelsea: their tickets are even more expensive than ones for Stamford Bridge. For the cheap seats, anyway
Verdict: Chelsea are worse

4. Cockroaches
❑ Better than Chelsea: they may be revolting, but at least they can be crushed by most opponents
❑ Just as bad as Chelsea: because they spend all their time on the floor
❑ Worse than Chelsea: because they'll still be around in a thousand years, whereas Mourinho presumably won't
Verdict: Chelsea are better

Oh f*ck!
le feuque... el farc
rrco

APRIL

League chiefs get into the spirit of April Fool's day by appointing Mike Pike, Bob Pollock and Eric Mackrell and Messrs Laws, Law and Lawson as the match officials at Coventry and Sheffield Wednesday respectively ... Reading chairman John Madejski thinks that Steve Coppell is a better manager than Jose Mourinho. "Girl" friend Cilla Black doesn't comment ... Alan Curbishley blames England job speculation for Charlton's poor run. So there's this speculation every year is there? ... Jack Straw shows US Secretary of State a good time at Ewood Park ... Red and yellow cards to be sponsored by a football-themed poker website from next season ... Man Utd branded "double dealers", geddit?, after they pull out of a proposed sponsorship deal with gambling firm Mansion ... Levski Sofia owner brands ref Mike Riley "a British homosexual" and threatens legal action after Riley sends off Sofia midfielder Cedric Bardon in their defeat to Schalke ... Cardiff skipper Darren Purse tells Swansea's Lee Trundle to "grow up" after the striker parades in a T-shirt showing a Swansea fan urinating on a Cardiff shirt and waves a flag reading "fuck off Cardiff" at the LDV Final ... "One Premiership manager said to me that he was the worst referee in the league and he wasn't wrong," says Paul Jewell as he strikes Phil Dowd from his Christmas card list ... Swedish equality ombudsman Claes Borgstrom says Sweden should pull out of the World Cup in protest at extra World Cup brothels being set up ... Sunderland's Kevin Kyle scalds his testicles after his eight-month-old son Max kicks a jug of boiling water over him. A former lover reveals the full extent of the tragedy. Apparently he is very well endowed ... Zlatan Ibrahimovic isn't impressed at being subbed by Fabio Capello at Treviso, telling the boss to "fuck off" in Croatian, Swedish, Italian and English. An understanding Capello insists "he is like a racehorse – highly strung but capable of winning us anything" ... David Sullivan apologises for his "I don't like footballers" rant ... Lee Trundle and Swansea team mate Alan Tate arrested on public order charges ... Trevor Brooking jets off to watch the US Masters in Augusta as a guest of Hammers fan Paul McGinley ... Wayne Rooney hires a dog trainer after his pooch keeps pebble-dashing Prestbury every morning ... Mars changes the name of its signature product to "Believe" to back England during the World Cup. "Heroic failure due to some foreign cheats and dodgy penalties fault" was thought too long ... Neil Ruddock stars as Neil

Diamond in *Celebrity Stars in Their Eyes* ... Brazil boss Carlos Alberto Parreira lifts the sex ban he originally imposed to win the 1994 World Cup. "Sex is welcome," he says. "Sex is fine". Sven agrees ... Harry Redknapp explains the secret behind Portsmouth's resurgent form. It's down to team spirit but not all his bonding experiments have gone down too well. A trip to the Billy Joel musical *Movin' Out* was not universally acclaimed. "A few of them weren't impressed with the idea," he says. "They were like 'are you having a laugh?'" A laugh? Only at the ticket prices ... The FA asks Paul Jewell to explain his assertion that Phil Dowd was "incompetent". An unrepentant Jewell adds, "Stevie Wonder would have given that free kick" ... Jose Mourinho refuses to go on *Parkinson* as the press plays up the possibility of Manchester United catching them. But that's not the reason. He's come over all Coleen on that score: "Bird flu scares me more than Man Utd," he insists ... Sunderland (four points at home all season) versus Fulham (no away wins) is officially the worst fixture in the 14-year history of the Premiership ... Tony Blair trains with Spurs, Brentford and Fulham players at the launch of the "Kickz" scheme to combat anti-social behaviour, but obviously not illiteracy ... Sheree Murphy judges "the best-dressed lady award" at the Grand National ... Blackburn's Aaron Mokoena is banned from driving for 12 months and fined £3,000 after admitting driving without insurance and while disqualified ... Coventry defender Ady Williams thinks there should be three whistles available when City take on Wolves as "both Incey and Wisey like to referee the match" ... A peasant with an impenetrable accent fails to show due respect in Frodsham, as Djibril Cisse reports: "Steven Gerrard teases me sometimes. When I come back from the showers he's wearing my clothes. I have funny underwear like zebra prints, so he puts them on." Footballers, eh? Spend half their time in the nude and are happy to put on someone else's warm underpants for a laugh but gay men, according to Tony Cascarino, make them "uncomfortable" ... Vinnie Jones is beaten by Martina Navratilova in the Hollywood Grand Prix motor race ... Gareth Southgate tells Sven to sort out England's problem gamblers. Surely penalty takers would be a better place to start ... Sir Bobby Robson has surgery after a skiing accident ... Tony Adams reveals one of Arsene Wenger's first moves in the Highbury hot seat was to ban pay-per-view porn on the team's away trips. Don't read on if you have a vivid imagination as Big Tone conjures up a graphic image of the Arsenal squad of 1996: "If players are exacting themselves quite a few times then it's going to have an effect on their physical condition". And their eyesight? ... Huddersfield's Danny Schofield booked for diving for the third time this season ... Underground Ernie's Walkers' Crisps are probed by Watchdog after complaints about salt and fat levels. Not to mention cheese ... Thierry Henry signs a new contract – dumping Nike for Reebok ... Malcolm Glazer calls Manchester United "a wonderful franchise" and launches a thousand lame "soccerball" gags ... An England player is alleged to have lost £37,000 on a single hand the night before England's 4-1 thrashing in Denmark. With stakes like that perhaps it's appropriate that the game of choice is brag ... Bayern Munich's Uli Hoeness says that it is inevitable that Michael Ballack will move to Chelsea at the end of his contract. "Michael did not want to learn a new language or culture but a new currency," he says ...

Managers of the month
APRIL
Who won the awards:

PREMIERSHIP
Harry Redknapp (Portsmouth)
Give him a couple of months to bed all those January signings in and what do you get? He's only gone and bleedin' done it, hasn't he? Four wins and two draws fires Pompey out of the relegation zone as Pedro Mendes can't stop scoring, Alexandre Gaydamak can't stop looking relieved, and Rupert Lowe can't stop kicking his filing cabinet.

CHAMPIONSHIP
Billy Davies (Preston North End)
Five wins in six gets Kamara purring about Preston's chances in May. "They head to the play-offs as the form team in the Championship." Immediate elimination all but secured, then.

LEAGUE ONE
Gary Johnson (Bristol City)
You can see the film pitch now. Big city club, on its uppers. Tried every trick in the book to get back where it belongs. Finally, along comes a young stranger to save the day but first he has to win his public over. It's a rocky road and at times it looks touch and go but at last the saviour prevails and is bequeathed the coveted silver Coke grail.

LEAGUE TWO
Ian Atkins (Torquay)
Four victories on what is known as the bounce mean the Atkins diet is more like a feast.

Who should have won the award:
David O'Leary (Aston Villa)
Okay, his record for the month shows only one win, four defeats and a draw but what a victory. By beating Birmingham City 3-1 to do the double over the Blues and escape the West Midlands relegation curse means that he achieved both of his seasonal objectives and did enough to hang onto his job. If not for long. A Holte End banner reads "We're not fickle, we just don't like you". Doug Ellis agrees.

Fired!
We're a long way through the season, time enough for Kevan Broadhurst to have arrived at Walsall and, in this month, to have departed again having successfully achieved relegation. John Cornforth, appointed by Torquay in January and also departing, lasted one month longer.

Kevan Broadhurst (Walsall)
Steve Bleasdale (Peterborough)
David Tuttle (Millwall)
John Cornforth (Torquay United)

STATISTICS
Top scorers (league only):

Thierry Henry (Arsenal) – 24
Ruud Van Nistelrooy (Man Utd) – 21
Darren Bent (Charlton) – 18
Frank Lampard (Chelsea) – 16
Wayne Rooney (Man Utd) – 16
Robbie Keane (Tottenham) – 16

Top performers:

Most shots on target: **Rooney** (Man Utd) – 73
Most shots off target: **Rooney** (Man Utd) – 74
Most shots without scoring:
Musampa (Man City) – 40
Most shots per goal: **Stead** (Sunderland) – 51
Most free-kicks won:
Luis Boa Morte (Fulham) – 100

Match of the month
MIDDLESBROUGH 4
STEAU BUCHAREST 2

In which we discovered: 1) Massimo Maccarone is alive, well and justifying his £8.1m transfer fee as a makeshift substitute right winger. 2) When forced to chase a game, the England assistant coach does not chuck on Owen Hargreaves and Phil Neville or their Boro equivalents Ray Parlour and Doriva but lobs on strikers instead. Who was holding who back, Sven? 3) It's amazing what morning headlines proclaiming Big Phil Scolari has been appointed as the new England manager can make you do to keep your name in the frame. 4) If you can antagonise Mark Viduka sufficiently he doesn't exactly burst out of his shirt and turn green but he does break into a sweat. 5) Eindhoven can sound like paradise when said in a Teesside accent.

Top of the table

		P	W	D	L	F	A	GD	Pts
1	**CHELSEA**	36	29	4	3	72	20	52	91
2	**MANCHESTER UNITED**	37	24	8	5	68	34	34	80
3	**LIVERPOOL**	37	24	7	6	54	24	30	79
4	**TOTTENHAM HOTSPUR**	37	18	11	8	52	36	16	65
5	**ARSENAL**	36	18	7	11	61	28	33	61

Bottom of the table

		P	W	D	L	F	A	GD	Pts
16	**ASTON VILLA**	37	9	12	16	40	54	-14	39
17	**PORTSMOUTH**	37	10	8	19	36	59	-23	38
18	**BIRMINGHAM CITY**	37	8	10	19	28	49	-21	34
19	**WEST BROM**	37	7	8	22	29	56	-27	29
20	**SUNDERLAND**	36	2	6	28	23	66	-43	12

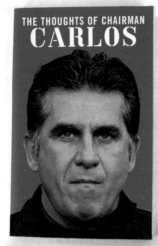

THE THOUGHTS OF CHAIRMAN CARLOS

CARLOS QUEIROZ'S
FOOTBALL HANDBOOK
MODULE 9

"SO CHELSEA HAVE beaten us and won the title but I don't think it's a coincidence that they started to win things when they put a coach from Portugal in charge. I wonder where Peter Kenyon got that idea from? I think we know. Yes Jose Mourinho, me, the head chef at Nandos and that transsexual from Big Brother are all Portuguese and we are all winners. Jose and I have many things in common. We have George Clooney hair. We like a nice coat. We believe in strong goalkeeping and sound defence. We are gamblers: we play the 4-5-1 or the "belt, braces and two pairs of underpants" system some of the time but in an instant will switch it to 4-3-3 or the "no one really understands how to play this way, who do you think we are bleedin' Ajax?" formation. We wouldn't know a decent left back if one came up and bit us on the bum. We like to take the best English talent the game has seen for years, let's call them Wayne and Joe, and take them out of the central areas and send them to shine by the margins on the touchline. And we've both been rubbish in Europe recently. Enough said. I don't think David Gill has to look much further when Sir Ferguson retires, do you?"

Theo's Diary

A funny-looking man has come to the playground a couple of times to monitor us. I think he must be a government inspector, although maybe he's a spy because he speaks in a very strange voice and doesn't sound English at all. I think he must be from around here though because whenever he's here all my English classmates go to talk to him but Thierry who's the head boy and from France doesn't seem very impressed. The funny man seems to look at me funny and I don't know why.

Alan Pardew's cheeseboard
Wensleydale, Red Leicester & Double Gloucester

I AM NOT THAT FUSSY which of these I get but it's got to be English cheese for me. If a cheeseboard does not reflect the produce of its home country, it devalues it however many continental competitions it wins. These cheeses reflect our character – they're stout, dependable, occasionally a bit thick, but they're our cheeses dammit and if we don't shout their merits from the rooftops, who will? We don't want platters over here consisting entirely of imported stuff, however tasty and beyond my price range they might be. And that doesn't make me a racist, just a proud Anglocurdophile.

Welcome to... Madrid

Michael Owen's move from Real Madrid to Newcastle doesn't fall under the classic definition of career progression, but it made the little striker happy. "People say to me, 'don't you miss the sun' but when I was out there I almost missed the rain," he said. "I did miss a lot about England. At Newcastle there are golf days and lunches out and jokes in the dressing room that I can actually understand. It's definitely where I belong. I'm a bit of an English homeboy at the end of the day."

"My first..."
Neil Warnock

Bastard fookin' Megson of a thing!!

MY FIRST BREATH I was born on 1 December 1948 in Sheffield.

MY FIRST WORDS I'm only guessing, but the first thing I ever said was probably something like "mummy", "daddy", or "oi, ref, you're a tosser."

MY FIRST HOBBY Writing poetry, definitely. I write about my players and the journeys we go on. I think it's important to have interests away from football. I think I'm really good at making things rhyme.

MY FIRST CLUB Chesterfield, then I stayed down in the lower leagues. I was never as good as my colleagues.

MY FIRST PET My fish they live upon my farm. I think they help to keep me calm. "I like fish," I said once. "I find them relaxing." My fish they swim around and round, and make a funny bubbly sound. I play with them, and with my daughter. Though she doesn't live underwater.

MY FIRST TOUCHLINE BAN There's one I got back in 2000, but since then my language's coarsened. I got another in 2003 and referees still persecute me. There came a third in May this year, but still I don't live in fear.

MY FIRST PROMOTION Was with Scarborough in 1987. To me success is a taste of heaven. I've also been up with Notts County and Huddersfield, but only in Sheffield have my true talents been revealed.

MY FIRST TRACTOR You could say I've got some unusual interests, and my antique tractor's one of them. It's almost 60 years old. "I've got an old tractor," I've said. "Not a big one. We've got a bit of land in Cornwall and I potter about." I appear to have stopped talking in rhyming couplets, which is a bonus as frankly that joke was wearing a bit thin.

MY FAVOURITE FILM I like to cry at films. "I am a softie," I said. "I love soppy films, anything with children in it." This can present problems when I'm watching DVDs our scout has put together of the best young talent. You can't help but shed a tear.

MY FIRST RELEGATION Now, none of that talk. We'll need to be positive if we're going to make it in the top flight. Did I tell you about the time I was offered the Chelsea job?

MY FIRST JOB I TURNED DOWN AND HAVEN'T STOPPED TALKING ABOUT SINCE Do you know I once said no to Chelsea? I did, you know. "I'm not really a London person," I explained. No, it doesn't make a lot of sense to me either.

THE HARD SELL

SCENE: Brian Barwick interviewing Sam Allardyce

Brian Barwick: (sotto voce) "Oh well, I suppose we'd better see him ... Ah Sam, come in. Now why do you think you should be England manager?"

Sam Allardyce: "Well, please read these dossiers, watch this Powerpoint presentation, listen to these testimonials, inspect these qualifications and shuffle through this Playlist."

Barwick: "But you've never won the league."

Allardyce: "Neither did Taylor, or Venables, or Hoddle or Keegan. It's impossible to win the title unless you're at one of the big four clubs and they don't employ English managers."

Barwick: "Aha! Do you see my dilemma? We want what's best for England and if an Englishman is not good enough for them, why should he be good enough for the FA?"

Allardyce: "Because the whole point of the FA is to promote English talent."

Barwick: "No, our job is to do what's best for English football and that means getting someone in who will play attractively and win matches."

Allardyce: "But that's me. I'm your man."

Barwick: "Some of our committee don't think you play attractive football."

Allardyce: "My England team would play in a different way to my Bolton team."

Barwick: "But would you be able to handle the egos?"

Allardyce: "Why don't you ask El Hadji Diouf or Fernando Hierro or Jay-Jay Okocha?"

Barwick: "Most impressive. Well, we'll look into it, thank you."

Allardyce: "So, I'll wait to hear from you."

Barwick: "Well, you can wait if you want to."

Allardyce: "So I haven't got the job?"

Barwick: "No. We've always had someone else in mind. Anyone else really. In fact, we've been deliberately wasting your time"

Allardyce: "I see..."

APRIL

123

(Continued from p.99)

PROPOSALS

So you've found your girl, you've had a few dates, now you want to hurry up and have some children before any of your team-mates start thinking that you're a homosexual. You may at this point be considering marriage, but you should put some thought into how – and where – you make your proposal. Some of us might prefer the spur-of-the-moment charm of Wayne Rooney, who proposed to Coleen in a garage forecourt, but most women want something a little more finely crafted than that.

Ashley Cole proposed, with the aid of a £50,000 diamond ring, in the footballers' playground of Dubai. She also gave him a diamond ring but he broke it. "When I was out I knocked the ring and the stone fell out. I don't think Cheryl was too happy but in the end she forgave me." Touchingly, he had asked her father for permission first. "He thought it was a big wind-up and that it wasn't me," he said. "In the end he realised it was for real and gave me his blessing. I was so relieved." It was certainly an improvement on his first declaration of love, which apparently came while they were watching television. "When you find the right person you know they're The One and you just want to be with them forever," he says. "That's how it is with Cheryl." Harry Kewell proposed to Sheree Murphy in the Maldives, a long way from where they met – Leeds nightclub Majestyk.

Rangers' Nacho Novo proposed to Donna Clark, who previously went out with his one-time team-mate Ross Mathieson, at a posh Italian restaurant in Glasgow, though she got embarrassed as he got on bended knee. "The restaurant was packed and I didn't want the extra attention, so when I saw him kneeling down I yelled: 'Stop! The answer's yes!' I'm quite a private person and I didn't want any more fuss. Half the restaurant was already staring at us." He bought a £6,000 white gold and diamond engagement ring, and bought a ring for himself while he was at it. "I took Donna to our favourite Italian restaurant for a meal," Novo said. "When we arrived, I had arranged for the staff to present her with a bunch of flowers. Her face lit up as the waiter walked through with them – but this turned to shock when she saw what was hidden in the bouquet. To be honest, I was expecting Donna to say no."

Steven Gerrard designed his engagement ring himself, took it home and hid it in his daughter's blanket. "I pulled it out and he just asked me," she said. "I was wearing my pyjamas but I'm happy it was like that. I'd have died if he'd done it in a restaurant."

But a romantic proposal doesn't necessarily mean married bliss: Swedish goalkeeper Magnus Hedman lit 250 candles around his house to create the mood he wanted when he proposed to Magdalena but they started divorce proceedings this year, two wackily-named children later (Lancelot and Avalon, since you ask).

STAGS

Not for footballers the weekend in Tallinn or the alcohol-fuelled outing to gimmicky school-disco nightclubs. Craig Bellamy's stag, for example, involved a group of 15 mates jetting to Las Vegas for the weekend at a cost of £20,000. Former Chelsea star Jody Morris took his friends to Hertfordshire's exclusive Grove Hotel where, according to "a witness", "they were guzzling champagne, beer and wine and acting like morons". Inevitably, it ended with the police being called after Rio Ferdinand was spotted "squirting people with a fire extinguisher" and Morris apparently "urinated in a plant pot". Barry Ferguson's 15-man trip to Portugal didn't quite go according to plan, as they were thrown out of their lavish Algarve hotel after two days and forced to move somewhere more down-at-heel. "We didn't once stop drinking," the Scotland star says.

WEDDINGS

There's an element of one-upmanship here. Every wedding must be bigger and more expensive than the last or *OK!* and *Hello!* won't be interested in buying the exclusive rights to publish the pictures. Occasionally a brave player will decide to buck the trend for flashy weddings. "We don't want a big affair," Ashley Cole said a few months before his big day, while Cheryl added: "We're not going to do a mag deal. We just want it to be a quiet affair with everyone we love there." Their commitment to avoid selling their pictures to a magazine sadly lasted only until *OK!* offered them £1million and before they knew it they had a couple of hundred guests, were flying American soul singers in to entertain the crowd and were having a diamante wedding outfit knocked up for their pet chihuahua Buster. Really. Cheryl's pop star chums provided the glamour although other footballers need to find their own – Craig Bellamy invited football-loving Rod Stewart. Of course you can avoid the tabloid frenzy entirely by doing it abroad – Danny Murphy married in Barbados and Harry Kewell in Las Vegas – in the same chapel used by Shirley Bassey, Richard Gere and, er, Telly Savalas, where the cost of a wedding starts at a distinctly un-Beckham-esque $75. Watch out for cunning locals – after Bellamy's wedding his party were kept in the church until they handed over their loose change to onlookers. This is apparently a local tradition in the Welsh town of St Brides-super-Ely, although it sounds quite like robbery to us. (Continued p.140)

WHY THE FA CUP IS STILL MAGIC

AS EVERYONE KNOWS, the magic of the FA Cup has become a little less powerful in recent years. And then there was Steven Gerrard in 2006. As the final whistle approached the midfielder couldn't walk. He was a hobbling, miserable invalid. Only two things could have inspired someone in his condition to sprint 20 yards and still leave their legs bursting with enough energy to propel the ball 40 yards into the goal at absurd speed. One of them is hot chocolate brownies with vanilla ice cream, and the other is magic. We're pretty sure it wasn't the brownies.

If there was nothing special about the FA Cup then:

1. Every game of the season would be prefaced by the teams walking out of the tunnel to be met by misfiring fireworks in big black boxes.

2. Every game would be followed by an open-top bus parade through the centre of town, complete with kids climbing trees to get the best view of their heroes.

3. The PA at every league ground would play 'Rockin' All Over the World' after each game, even though it is 30 years old and has nothing to do with sport.

4. All matches would take place at a neutral venue as inconvenient as possible for both teams; train tickets would sell out and anyone attempting to drive will spend four and a half hours after the game exiting the host city.

5. Before each game, members of both teams would be introduced to someone in a suit who's never been to a football stadium before, but who may play an important role with a multinational soft drinks conglomerate.

6. Stalls will spring up outside every ground, from which enterprising merchandisers will flog Chester v Hereford commemorative scarves to grateful punters.

7. Every single game, even Port Vale v Scunthorpe, would be watched live via satellite by 14 billion people in 143 countries.

8. All games would be played in the month of May, but only when the sun shines.

9. There would be an enormous increase in tourism to Nottinghamshire as fans of teams visiting Mansfield decide to "make a weekend of it".

10. At the end of every match the players would be interrupted as they make their way off the field and forced by men in dark blazers and even darker glasses to pose behind large and heavily sponsored advertising hoardings.

Continued from p.114

Nightclubs

ODYSSEY, MANCHESTER

21 Ashley Road, Altrincham WA14 2DP
Tel. 0161 928 5959 / www.odysseybar.co.uk

The website suggests it's got "real 'wow' factor", and you're likely to be making astonished exclamations once you see their price list (so big that their most expensive cocktail comes with a free diamond ring). It's "uber-contemporary", just so you know. The VIP suite is called Q and is "tactile, textured, intimate and interesting", which makes it sounds like a toy you might give your cat.

Tabloid tales

Wayne Rooney caught on CCTV in the kitchen getting friendly with Emily Fountain, before the camera was covered up for six minutes, 22 seconds. In the same month, November 2005, Rio Ferdinand came here to celebrate a 1-0 win over Chelsea. When a barman asked for a picture Ferdinand is alleged to have responded: "Why can't people like you just fuck off?"

  £

ONE CENTRAL STREET, MANCHESTER

1 Central Street M2 5RW / Tel. 0161 211 9000
www.onecentralstreet.co.uk

This won Theme Magazine's best interior design award in 2002. It's that good.

Tabloid tales

Wayne Rooney was chased into the toilets by the boyfriend of a woman whose bottom he pinched, who sadly turned out to be a reporter on a tabloid newspaper. Rooney was also seen smoking.

TIGER TIGER, MANCHESTER

The Printworks, Withy Grove, M4 2BS
Tel. 0161 385 8080 / www.tigertiger-manch.co.uk

Growing nationwide chain, where drinks and food are cheap enough for normal people to spend the night. Nevertheless, it's a popular haunt for people who really should be somewhere a little more exclusive.

Tabloid tales

Cristiano Ronaldo seems to be a regular. Wayne Rooney had a stand-up row with an aggressive Everton fan here shortly after his move to Manchester United. "I never laid a finger on him," Rooney said. "He landed three punches," said the Everton fan.

PROHIBITION, MANCHESTER

2-10 St Mary's Street, M3 2LB / 0870 220 3026

Cocktail bar and eatery (burgers, fish & chips, not much for athletes) with branches in Nottingham and Leeds, it "offers a full-on party atmosphere", which is probably why people come here for their parties.

Tabloid Tales

Final destination for Blackburn's 2005 fancy dress Christmas party. Their first, incidentally, was Mulligan's Irish Pub. Wings' Chinese restaurant came between them. A classy affair, by all accounts.

Continued p.142

APRIL

Balls

127

Whhoooooooooosh!

MAY

Our quadrennial obsession with metatarsals begins when Wayne Rooney is injured. Tord Grip, for one, has a sense of déjà vu. "It happened before with Beckham," he accurately points out, "and now it's happening again"… Steven Gerrard is just as upbeat: "It is impossible to have a successful World Cup without Wayne." Hmm, funny how Brazil usually manage it … David Beckham narrowly avoids serious injury after an Osasuna fan throws a coffee pot at the England skipper. He polishes it and places it back in its correct position on the sideboard … *The Sun* asks readers to sing a modified version of the Aretha Franklin classic to aid Rooney's recovery "I Say A Little Prayer For Roo" – that should do it … Steve McClaren outs his affair with Middlesbrough secretary Karen Nelson having allegedly taken Max Clifford's advice to forestall a leak timed to coincide with his appointment as England manager … Jose Mourinho throws two Premiership medals and his blazer into the Stamford Bridge crowd. Roman, you can't buy class like that … Port Vale announce that Robbie Williams' reward for his investment will see "a stand, a refreshment kiosk or a hospitality room" named after him. The Bovril option looks the likeliest … Southampton fans show their displeasure at chairman Rupert Lowe with a "pants protest" after placards and banners are banned … Birmingham's co-owner David Sullivan brands his players arrogant: "they will blame everyone but themselves if we get relegated". That's the problem with co-owners. With some clubs you have to listen to twice the amount of opinions thought up when ranting at the limo driver … Gary Neville rows with United fans who branded the team "a fucking disgrace" after the goalless draw with Middlesbrough … Rooney adopts a Michael Jackson gambit (steady!) and sleeps in oxygen tent … Underground Ernie vows to keep his forthcoming divorce "friendly" for the sake of his children … A 75-foot poster of Alan Shearer faces removal from St James' Park as Toon officials forgot to get planning permission … Sven starts work on Plan B … FA risks the wrath of the England players' wives by telling them they can only take one suitcase each to Germany after the Euro 2004 debacle when their mule-train of Louis Vuitton luggage wouldn't fit on the plane. Sadly they forgot to put a limit on how much the WAGs could bring back … The objective Claude Makelele says that "Chelsea are the best team in the world". The lessons on humility on that midseason trip to Lourdes clearly weren't wasted … Steve Claridge is left marooned on 999 senior appearances after Walsall boss Richard Money drops him from the Saddlers' final game of the season ... BSkyB win the latest Premiership TV contract providing Andy Gray with players to swoon over and referees to slaughter for the next three years ... France's team slogan for the World Cup, "liberté, égalité, Jules Rimet", it is revealed, was penned by an England fan from Telford. Not Julian Cope, presumably ... Blackburn's Ryan Nelsen plays for 30 minutes with a hairline fracture of the leg ... Ruud van Nistelrooy storms out of Old Trafford after being told Giuseppe Rossi would start ahead of him: The following day it emerges that far from storming out, he was sent home for attitude problems. Being replaced by a 19-year-old can do that ... Arsenal claim fourth place in the Premiership by dint of winning at Highbury as Spurs lose at West Ham ... Tottenham "smell a rat" after 10 players are alleged to have suffered food poisoning in the run up to the match. Dodgy lasagne is named as the prime suspect ... Wigan's Pascal Chimbonda hands in a written transfer request to Paul Jewell as he leaves the pitch at Highbury. Pre-match ritual – right sock first, check, jockstrap, check, left sock, check, shorts, check, boots, check, sock-ties, check, shirt, check, stick of Wrigleys, check, transfer request, natch. "The timing is diabolical," storms Dave Whelan ... Rooney is having to relieve the boredom of his oxygen tank by having hip-hop pumped in as well ... Prince William is given leave from army training to attend England's World Cup matches ... Spurs demand a replay due to "lasagnegate" ... Felix Magath, Bayern Munich's coach, misses the team's championship winning party after sampling too much of Bavaria's finest. "I had more than one too many," he admits ... Double interregnum England boss Howard Wilkinson describes Notts County's last day escape from relegation as "like being on death row in an American jail. You are waiting for the door handle to turn not knowing if it's a reprieve or your final meal before being executed" ... A demob happy Sven springs a major surprise by picking 17-year-old Theo Walcott in his World Cup squad despite never seeing him play. "It's my biggest gamble," he admits. Bigger than telling a cockney in a white sheet that you'd like to manage Villa? ... It is now alleged that Ruud van Nistelrooy was sent home from Old Trafford for telling Cristiano Ronaldo that Carlos Queiroz was his father. Ronaldo's father died in September ... Spurs withdraw threat of legal action over ok-it-wasn't-the-lasagne-but-we-still-had-food-poisoning-gate ... QPR chairman tells court how he was forced to sign over club shares with a gun pointed at his head. Future robot artiste Peter Crouch is known as "Chesney" by his Liverpool teammates as he's always singing "The One And Only" ... Leeds beat Preston in the second leg of the play-offs to qualify for the final and are quick to remind Billy Davies of his touchline "job done" celebration by scrawling, "How's about that for job done you Scotch !*%@" in the Away dressing rooms at Deepdale. Terrible etiquette. Scotch is a drink ... Watford boss Aidy Boothroyd sparks a 20-man brawl in the play-off second leg with Crystal Palace. Adrian, really ... Theo Walcott reveals his ambitions are to pass his driving test, buy a VW Golf and win the World Cup ... Freddie Kanouté says English football is "second rate" ... Wayne Bridge is injured after a nightclub brawl ... Theo Walcott admits Michael Owen's 1998 wonder goal against Argentina went unseen by him as it was past his bedtime ... Former Wales international Leighton James takes a new job as a lollipop man...

Managers of the month

MARCH

Who won the awards:

There aren't any as it's time for the seasonal gongs to be handed out. And the sole criterion, it seems, is finishing top of the league.

PREMIERSHIP

Jose Mourinho (Chelsea)

Graciously accepts the award saying he feels his achievements are not properly understood: "I have been here for two years, we are champions and I have won manager of the month two times in two years." They probably know that if Jose gets an award more than once, he just gives it away.

CHAMPIONSHIP

Steve Coppell (Reading)

The League Managers' Association gave him the divisional title and their top award, the manager of the year Waterford crystal vase, probably antagonising Jose even further.

LEAGUE ONE

Steve Tilson (Southend)

Leading the revival of Essex football and holding off Phil Parkinson's Colchester to win League One by three points, Tilson won an LMA award for the second successive season. His entire playing career was spent in the Cowslip county at Witham Town, Southend and Canvey Island. Buy a travelcard, man.

LEAGUE TWO

Paul Simpson (Carlisle)

Twelve points adrift at the foot of the table when he took charge in 2003, he remodelled the once-Michael Knighton benighted club and kick-started Michael Bridges' career after six years of injuries.

Who should have won the award:

Stuart Pearce (Manchester City)

Losing 21 of 38 league games to finish 15th in the Premiership, and still it "would be absolute

folly" to rule himself out of the race for the England job. Never has a coach boasting a win-loss-draw record of 27-30-19 come so close too. Proof that a nice line in deadpan modesty and a handful of ants down the tracksuit pants before taking to the touchline can do wonders for one's profile.

Fired!

The season comes to an end, and so do a large number of contracts. At this point you pay for a disappointing season, pausing only to release a carefully worded statement praising the board and mentioning that you've "taken the club as far as you can".

So much action on the managerial roundabout this month, we've had to print it really small.

Johan Boskamp (Stoke), Brian Little (Tranmere), Paul Stephenson (Hartlepool), Barry Hunter (Rushden & Diamonds), Alan Curbishley (Charlton), Danny Wilson (MK Dons), Joe Royle (Ipswich), Steve McClaren (Middlesbrough), Steven Thompson (Yeovil), Iffy Onuora (Swindon), Iain Dowie (Crystal Palace), Keith Alexander (Lincoln), Gudjon Thordarson (Notts County), John Gorman (Wycombe), Colin Calderwood (Northampton), Martin Allen (Brentford), Russell Slade (Grimsby)

Hired!

Dennis Wise (Swindon), Iain Dowie (Charlton), Paul Hart (Rushden & Diamonds), Richard Money (Walsall), Keith Alexander (Peterborough), Nigel Spackman (Millwall), Colin Calderwood (Nottingham Forest)

END OF SEASON STATISTICS

Top scorers (league only):

Henry (Arsenal) – 27
Van Nistelrooy (Manchester United) – 21
D Bent (Charlton) – 18
Lampard (Chelsea) – 16
Rooney (Man Utd) – 16
Keane (Tottenham) – 16

MAY

Balls

Match of the month
WATFORD 3 LEEDS UNITED 0

In which we discovered: 1) "Aidy" is a perfectly acceptable name for an adult. If he's on the winning side. 2) If one of your players blanches, ducks and looks as though he's had a heart attack when the pre-match fireworks explode, as with Leeds's Liam Miller, you probably know it's not your day. 3) This match is worth £20m or £30m or £40m, depending on which newspaper you read. 4) Even if Watford don't hoof it, most commentators are too lazy to look beyond "Hornets=Graham Taylor=Route One" in their bumper book of team stereotypes. 5) If David Healy is good enough to humiliate England by scoring against Neville, Ferdinand, Terry and Cole why is he only good enough to appear for Leeds as a 70th-minute substitute?

Final table

	Team	P	W	D	L	F	A	GD	Pts
1	CHELSEA	38	29	4	5	72	22	50	91
2	MANCHESTER UNITED	38	25	8	5	72	34	38	83
3	LIVERPOOL	38	25	7	6	57	25	32	82
4	ARSENAL	38	20	7	11	68	31	37	67
5	TOTTENHAM HOTSPUR	38	18	11	9	53	38	15	65
6	BLACKBURN ROVERS	38	19	6	13	51	42	9	63
7	NEWCASTLE UNITED	38	17	7	14	47	42	5	58
8	BOLTON WANDERERS	38	15	11	12	49	41	8	56
9	WEST HAM UNITED	38	16	7	15	52	55	-3	55
10	WIGAN ATHLETIC	38	15	6	17	45	52	-7	51
11	EVERTON	38	14	8	16	34	49	-15	50
12	FULHAM	38	14	6	18	48	58	-10	48
13	CHARLTON ATHLETIC	38	13	8	17	41	55	-14	47
14	MIDDLESBROUGH	38	12	9	17	48	58	-10	45
15	MANCHESTER CITY	38	13	4	21	43	48	-5	43
16	ASTON VILLA	38	10	12	16	42	55	-13	42
17	PORTSMOUTH	38	10	8	20	37	62	-25	38
18	BIRMINGHAM CITY	38	8	10	20	28	50	-22	34
19	WEST BROMWICH ALBION	38	7	9	22	31	58	-27	30
20	SUNDERLAND	38	3	6	29	26	69	-43	15

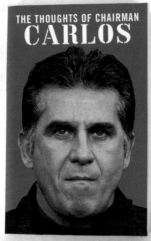

THE THOUGHTS OF CHAIRMAN
CARLOS

CARLOS QUEIROZ'S
FOOTBALL HANDBOOK
MODULE 10

THE END OF THE SEASON is a time to take stock, the draw breath, to move two steps back and seek a better view of things. From here, we can see where we have gone wrong, and where we have been proved right. And I must admit, the view is extremely good. I have therefore instructed the players that we must take two steps back more often next season. Only once we have retreated can we attack. A glance at the league table reveals our troubles. No one scored more goals than us – if anything, we had too many – but our defence was not sturdy enough. We mastered the dark art of attack but without the defence to shed light upon it we remained blind to the truth. Two steps back next season. I have instructed Sir Alex to rid the squad of its greatest striker. He will be needed no more. Two steps back. I think we shall enjoy the view. "

me!

Theo's Dia[ry]

The funny-looking man has asked me to go on summer holiday with him. I think it's a bit weird but Mum and Dad are really happy and Dad's going to come with me and so is my girlfriend Melanie even though she's got exams. I don't get it because all I've been doing for ages is watching other people play football but at least I know I must be very good at it. If you ask me I think my dad's better because he's been doing it for like 50 years and has done so much practice that the sofa has moulded itself to fit his butt cheeks.

Neil Warnock's cheeseboard
Red Leicester & Wensleydale

I CAN'T STAND THEM ON THEIR OWN but when the wife chops them up into red and white strips and sticks 'em on my plate, it's ace. Nah, I can't stand white cheese, or bloody Leeds cheese as I call it, and I won't give that blue and white muck house room. I like a hunk of red next to a hunk of white; let it fester for a few days until it smells of old feet and it takes me right back to my chiropody days. Red, white and smelly. Champion!

Welcome to... Moscow

Maniche thought his career was going to go stellar after he won the 2004 Champions League with Porto and then drove Portugal to the Euro 2004 final, but he he ended up in the Russian capital. "I don't want to say bad things about a city which received me so well," he says. "I'm very close to my family and when they're unhappy, so am I. My family tried it for a month and didn't like it – and that was in the summer!"

Spurs Logic Puzzle

On the last day of the season Spurs were to take on West Ham needing to match Arsenal's result against Wigan to secure Champions League football. But at some point after they dined together on the night before the match 10 Spurs players started vomiting uncontrollably. Desperate requests for a postponement fell on deaf ears. Weakened, they slipped to defeat at Upton Park and their north London rivals stole their place in Europe's premier competition, and the £10m that goes with it. From the clues below, can you work out what each of these five people had for supper on that fateful evening and whether any of them should have a guilty conscience?

Clues:

1. I wouldn't touch that lasagne if I were you, it looks well dodgy. You'll need a particularly robust constitution if you're not going to regret it.

2. Arsenal's team dietician is very precise about what should be eaten by both players and coaches before matches, believing that a properly balanced meal coupled with the correct doses of dietary supplements will satisfy both the stomach and the soul.

3. 40-year-olds simply don't play Premiership football unless they have previously discovered a remedy for ageing.

4. As a manager, it is your responsibility to ensure that your team is fit, healthy and tactically prepared for every match. If, for any reason, that is not the case, you'll need to find someone else to blame. Consider, in this order, the league, the chairman, your least favourite player, your local rivals, or an international conspiracy led by a powerful Russian billionaire or, if you're employed by a powerful Russian billionaire, the referee.

5. Hammers striker Bobby Zamora made a point of mentioning afterwards that "Jermain Defoe looked sharp". Indeed, the quicksilver forward played a full 90 minutes at Upton Park, scoring a fine goal, and finished it looking as fresh as a daisy in spring.

6. Martin Jol wouldn't touch a salad. What do you think he is, a Frenchman?

Arsenal manager: ARSENE WENGER

Tottenham manager: MARTIN JO[L]

Spurs midfielder: MICHAEL CARRIC[K]

West Ham striker: TEDDY SHERINGHA[M]

Bench-bound Spurs forward JERMAIN DEFO[E]

WHAT TO DO

Desperately appeal for t[he] Premier League to do somethi[ng]

Keep drinking it for a few years un[til] you're back in the England tea[m]

A good night's rest and lo[ok] forward to the new da[y]

Drink luke-warm, salinated wat[er] and eat dry toa[st]

Poisoned team-mates = a rare place in th[e] starting line-up. Resolve to do it more oft[en]

A swig on my eternal youth potion before I we[nt] out for the night with an 18-year-o[ld] glamour mode[l]

WHAT THEY ATE

The same as what everyone el[se] had, hone[st]

A lovely beef lasag[ne]

A salad and my daily do[se] of creati[ne]

Whatever the gaffer told me

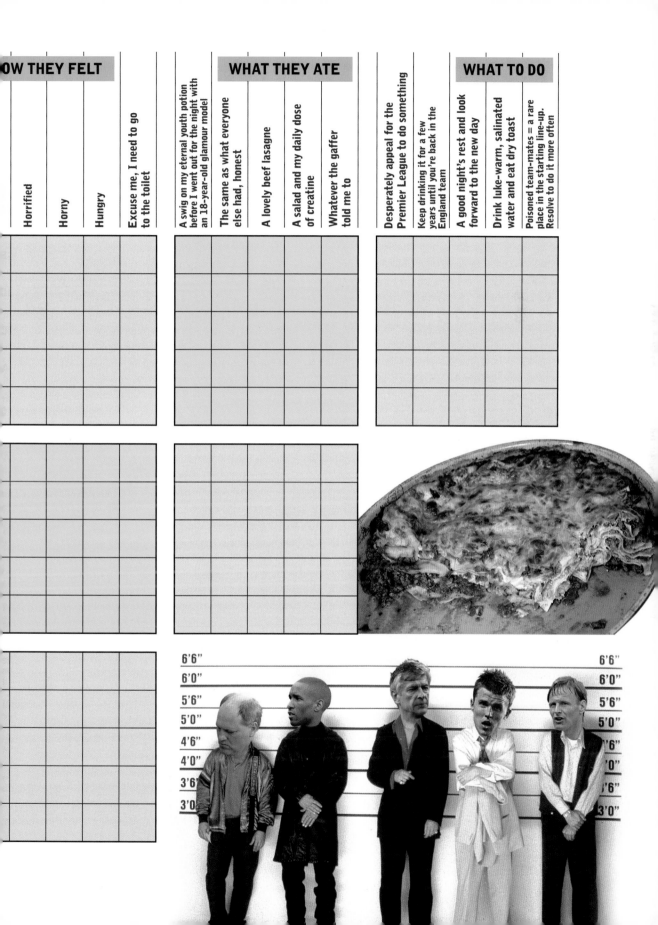

OW THEY FELT			
Horrified	Horny	Hungry	Excuse me, I need to go to the toilet

WHAT THEY ATE			
A swig on my eternal youth potion before I went out for the night with an 18-year-old glamour model	The same as what everyone else had, honest	A lovely beef lasagne	A salad and my daily dose of creatine	Whatever the gaffer told me to

WHAT TO DO			
Desperately appeal for the Premier League to do something	Keep drinking it for a few years until you're back in the England team	A good night's rest and look forward to the new day	Drink luke-warm, salinated water and eat dry toast	Poisoned team-mates = a rare place in the starting line-up. Resolve to do it more often

REVEALED:
How Barcelona won the European Cup

BARCELONA'S EUROPEAN CUP success was achieved thanks in part to the skill of their players and the dedication of their management team, but largely because of a single piece of high-tech gadgetry that is believed to be the first on the market to combine the ability to extract useful information about a team's opponents, in this case Arsenal, with the possible bonus of infecting them with rabies.

We are talking about the very latest development in the world of espionage, the most stunning technological advance to hit the world of sport since boots became so thin and whispy that you could break a metatarsal warming up and balls became so light and floaty that goalkeepers could complain all the time about them swerving too much in mid-air, and it's all encased a disguise so brilliant that – until this moment – nobody had realised what they had actually seen.

It was a robot rodent. The very latest model created by a Madrid-based technological firm and known as SpySquirrel2000™. And when it ran on to the pitch during Arsenal's semi-final against Villareal it fed Frank Rijkaard and his boys from Barcelona information picked up from the Highbury turf that led to their slightly-more-arduous-than-it-should-have-been victory over Arsenal's 10 men in the Stade de France. Here, in a *Balls!* world exclusive, we explain how it worked.

Using this information, Barcelona found out where their players should run and which of their opponents were most unfit. They knew what Arsene Wenger's tactics were and how to counteract them. They relied on their players' ability, they relied on their manager's motivational techniques, but they did not rely on chance. Here, for the first time, is proof.

Eyes: In fact these are tiny infra-red sensors, allowing it to send and receive information from up to 150 yards. It can also read bar codes accidentally left on bird feeders, which it transfers immediately to the SpySquirrel™ central databank and uploads the best method of getting at their contents, even if the bird feeder is supposed to be totally squirrelproof.

Ears: Long-range microphones capable of picking up sound from multiple sources. At the same time they can hear the instructions coming from Arsenal's bench, conversations between goalkeeper Jens Lehmann and his defence, and still retain sufficient computer power to pick up the soft thud of a falling conker.

Nose: Can smell fear from 50 paces. Remember, however, that squirrel paces are extremely short.

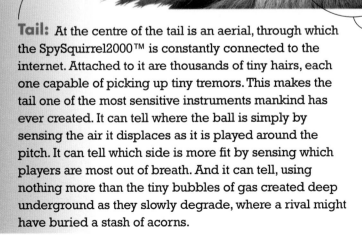

Tail: At the centre of the tail is an aerial, through which the SpySquirrel2000™ is constantly connected to the internet. Attached to it are thousands of tiny hairs, each one capable of picking up tiny tremors. This makes the tail one of the most sensitive instruments mankind has ever created. It can tell where the ball is simply by sensing the air it displaces as it is played around the pitch. It can tell which side is more fit by sensing which players are most out of breath. And it can tell, using nothing more than the tiny bubbles of gas created deep underground as they slowly degrade, where a rival might have buried a stash of acorns.

Legs: Squirrels may be small but they are extremely quick and astonishingly nimble. In two minutes on the pitch the SpySquirrel2000™ can give any defender the slip, sensing vulnerability and working out immediately where a player should run to cause most discomfort.

SIR ALEX FERGUSON'S
Dossier
+ + + + + + + May 2006 + + + + + + +

A canny manager never lets himself get marginalised. I didn't get where I am today, having grown up on the mean streets of Govan, by letting myself get pushed around by anyone. I might not look like a street brawler but you wouldn't want to get on the wrong side of me.

Or the right side of me, dammit. If I were you, I'd steer clear of either side of me. Just steer clear of me. D'you hear me, boy? Steer well clear. The surest way to the scrapheap is by coming up to me giving it the bad boy routine, slagging off my management style or your teammates to the papers or sticking it in a book. I had a player did that, name of Jaap Stam. Best defender in the world, he was, but I didn't think twice. Before he knew it he was out the door and onto the scrapheap. Didn't know what had hit him. Next thing he knew he was playing for AC Milan in the European Cup final. That's how far he fell, son.

There was another guy did something similar, name of Roy Keane. My midfield general for a decade, he was. The hardest man on the field, he was my eyes and my ears and my mouth and my nose. He was my heads and my shoulders and my knees and my toes, he was. But then he turned all big time Charlie on me, went on my own bloody TV station to give the lads a kicking. Before he knew it he was seeing out the last remnants of his career on a lucrative contract at Celtic, never to darken the door of Old Trafford again, except for money-spinning sold-out testimonial nights.

I could go on. Dammit, I will go on. Let me tell you about Paul Ince. He called himself The Guv'nor, a bloody ridiculous title. He thought he was a lot more important than he was. He reckoned the team revolved around him. Tosh. The only thing that was revolving was the door, and he was on his way out of it. He was a footballing pariah when he left here. No one would touch him. Except Internazionale, of course, and then Liverpool and Wolves.

You've probably heard of David Beckham. You've definitely seen his face. On every bloody advertising hoarding from Brighton to Blackpool, from Totnes to Tokyo, that man. There's nothing he couldn't sell. He was an incredible footballer, the best right foot I've ever seen. The crosses he could deliver, the free-kicks he could hit. Unbelievable. But then people started to mumble, though not round me you understand, that he was more important to the club than me, that the money men would never let him leave. Well we found out the truth of that, didn't we? He left, sure enough. To a crappy little club in Spain. And the money man left too, and what's his new club done since? Don't answer that.

So that's where we stand, Ruud. You're the best goalscorer this club has had since Denis Law, or so they say. Indispensable, or so they say. And you know what I do to indispensable players? That's right, sonny. I dispense with them. So you're out. Your career's over. You're going down. Pack your bags, you're no' wanted here. Oh, and Real Madrid are on the phone.

(Continued from p.125)

Romance

ROMANTIC GESTURES

David Beckham is good at these. "My wife is an amazing woman and I'm very proud of her," he says. He proved it by spending £20,000 flying her to England from Japan, having her picked up at the airport and taken to Blakes Hotel, where he'd hired a £950-a-night suite and filled it with flowers and gifts, before taking her to her favourite restaurant, Cipriani. Sadly, making romantic gestures often involves spending large amounts of money. Ashley Cole, him again, gave Cheryl Tweedy a £25,000 diamond bracelet for her 22nd birthday. "It's beautiful," she said. "He wanted to buy me lots of other things but I told him he didn't have to. I've got everything I want in life - I'm getting married to him." Bleeurgh. Outpourings of emotion can be humiliating, even for the supposedly grateful girl. "I get embarrassed if he gets soppy," says Alex Curran of Steven Gerrard. "For me romance is just us spending time together." Bleeurgh again. Some are less conventional. Claude Makelele's on-off partner Neomie Lenoir said: "He is very romantic. He would send me flowers at all times and said all the right things." So far so normal, but she continued: "The only thing that worried me was his obsession with pornography. He had hundreds of films and wanted to watch them all the time. I put up with them because I was in love with him."

DOMESTIC BLISS

The less said about the at-home habits of the nation's finest footballers the better. Here's a taster: "Steven puts the odd wash on, but it's usually a disaster because he puts all the coloureds in with the whites and everything comes out a big, grey mess," says Alex Curran. Footballer-turned-pundit Jamie Redknapp is more of a hit at home. "He does the nappies and the bathing," says his wife Louise. "I could leave the baby with him all day and night and not worry about him - although when I got home the house would be horrific!" Michael Owen, also married to someone called Louise, got out of the worst jobs after the birth of his daughter Gemma Rose. "I've been trying to get the hang of the nappies," he said. "It looks a bit technical for me at the moment." Owen also wheels out the trusty post-birth footballer's excuse for making the unlucky mum do all the hard work by adding that he "couldn't really afford to interrupt my sleep patterns".

TRUE LOVE

"I'm happy when Rob is happy and he is happy when I am happy," said former Miss Ireland finalist Claudine Palmer of her relationship with Robbie Keane. No, we've never heard anyone call him Rob before either. It's as a good a definition of love as we've found among football folk, and other long-term sufferers include Coleen, who says of life with Wayne Rooney: "We love each other and that means we'll be with each other as long as we're alive", and Cheryl "this is the man I'm going to have my babies with" Cole, wife of Ashley. "From the first day I saw her I knew that I would be with her for the rest of my life," he says. Bless.

WHEN LOVE GOES BAD

The quantity of wannabe FWs means that there is no such thing as job security. But if your man should stray, you can always take it out on him through the media, or by beating up his car, or by beating up his car and then telling the media. The Norwich striker Leon McKenzie found this out the hard way when he left his wife for a 23-year-old Spaniard, making his spurned partner Vanessa "so mad I smashed up his Mercedes with a hockey stick". Less violent, and only slightly less memorable, was the approach of Claude Makelele's Neomie Lenoir, who left the midfielder after she found out about his womanising and fell into the arms of the tabloid press. "Claude was a fantastic lover, and we enjoyed the best sex of our lives, but it was not enough for him," she says, tearfully displaying the £100,000 diamond-studded necklace he gave her. He gave an identical item to one of his lovers. "All he wanted to do was cheat on me with any other women he could find. He has disgraced himself, his family and Chelsea football club. All of us are utterly ashamed of him. He was the man I wanted to marry, but now I never want to see him again." Not, at least, until the World Cup, by which time she was back by his side. Becky Hendrie, ex-wife of serial womaniser Lee, summed up her experience succinctly: "Everybody thinks life as a footballer's wife is pure heaven – but mine turned to hell." She got her revenge by scratching the words "prick" and "wanker" onto his brand new £60,000 Porsche.

BEING FAMOUS

Finally, a story of our times. "Lilley-Ella and I went past the bus stop the other day and there was a big photograph of Steven in an advert for adidas," says Alex Curran. "She just said: 'Daddy'." If your child does the same, you probably need to ask your wife some searching questions.

Nightclubs

Continued from p.127

FANTASY BAR, MANCHESTER

140 Deansgate M3 2RP / 0161 835 1973
http://ztweb.com/fantasy

Not just a bar but a lap dancing club.

Tabloid tales

A favourite of Bolton's El-Hadji Diouf, apparently.
The spitting striker's most famous nightclub
incident saw him accused of assaulting the ex-
wife of his former Bolton team-mate Khalilou
Fadiga in a Dakar nightspot. He denied it, and
the pair came to an out of court settlement.

BRASINGAMENS, ALDERLEY EDGE, CHESHIRE

London Road SK9 7QD

A recent redesign makes it pleasing on the eye,
and a secret electronic side door to which only
top celebrities have access make it easy to
spirit away your companions without the
paparazzi noticing. At the very heart of
Cheshire's footballers' belt.

Tabloid tales

Once a favourite haunt of the Beckhams, it's still
frequently visited by Manchester's finest
footballers. And some City players, too. In 2005
the Rooneys allegedly had a screaming row that
brought the establishment to tabloid attention. "I
have never seen anything like it," said a
"witness". "This is an upmarket place and people
don't normally act like that." Rio Ferdinand, Wes
Brown and Roy Carroll were there too.

GARLANDS, LIVERPOOL

Dale Street L1 / Tel. 0151 709 9586
www.garlandsonline.co.uk

One for big nights out rather than casual
drinking, this gay bar is where footballers come
for their Christmas party.

Tabloid tales

Where Liverpool had their 2004 Christmas party
and Rangers theirs in 2005. "Franny Jeffers paid
for them all to get in," said the club's promoter,
adding: "He's been in a few times."

BABY BLUE, LIVERPOOL

Edward Pavilion, Albert Dock, L3 4AB
Tel. 0151 709 7097
www.lyceumgroup.co.uk/babyblue

A barrel-vaulted cavern on the Albert Dock, a
classy private member's bar that also offers
comedy and speed-dating. "You know how great
you are," they gasp. "Let someone else see it too."

Tabloid tales

Wayne Rooney's girlfriend Coleen McLoughlin
had a famously expensive night out there,
drinking Cristal champagne at £199 a bottle.

BABY CREAM, LIVERPOOL

Atlantic Pavilion, Albert Dock
tel. 0151 702 5826 / www.babycream.co.uk

They're all a bunch of babies in Liverpool. It used
to be the Beige Bar, and now it's Cream. Can you
see what they're doing there? It'll be White before

long. Anyway, we digress. A joint venture from the people behind the now-defunct Cream superclub and the moneymen behind Baby Blue, this is "an exciting new lounge bar restaurant concept". Check out the girls-only powder room, where the ladies can "check on their make-up and have girly chats over a glass of champagne". Their top-priced champagne, incidentally, costs £285.

Tabloid tales

Steve Finnan was spotted drinking here in March. Hold the front page.

ISIS, LIVERPOOL

Stonedale Retail Park, East Lancs. Road, L11 9BZ
tel. 0151 545 4800 / www.clubisis.co.uk

Brings a new meaning to the term "techno club" by being a club packed with technology. Yes, there's "an amazing state of the art lightshow" which turns the dance-floor into "a constant wash of colour". They've also got their own Hummer so you can arrive in (not very eco-friendly) style. It was once owned by George Michael, apparently. They say they "take a step back to a time of excess and glamour", neither of which is exactly foreign to Djibril Cissé.

Tabloid tales

Cisse turned DJ here to launch his "fashion" label Klubb 9 in March. Fellow players, including Steven Gerrard, Jamie Carragher and Peter Crouch, filled the dance-floor. None of them have been seen wearing his clothes though.

ALMA DE CUBA, LIVERPOOL

St Peter's Church, Seel Street L1 4AZ
Tel. 0151 709 7097 / www.alma-de-cuba.com

A Caribbean-themed bar in what used to be St Peter's Catholic church, retaining the original stained-glass windows.

Tabloid tales

Steven Gerrard's fiancee Alex Curran bought dinner for no less than seven friends in March, when out for a mid-pregnancy treat. This was also the venue for her 23rd birthday party. More remarkably, the *Mirror* reported Wayne Rooney being seen "holding the door open" for his girlfriend Coleen McLoughlin here in January. So popular with the city's footballers, even Xabi Alonso comes here. The food, apparently, is actually good.

COOPERAGE BAR, NEWCASTLE

32 The Close, Quayside, NE1 3RQ
Tel. 0191 232 8286
www.thecooperagenewcastle.co.uk

A beer-drinkers beerodrome, with Club Xcalibur upstairs if you accidentally packed your dancing shoes.

Tabloid tales

Where Craig Bellamy and his one-time lady friend, "curvy lapdancer" Mickala Jamil, went out one night and "things got so heated he dragged me off to the ladies four times". "We didn't even stop when some girls came in to fix their make-up," she reported.

THE WORKS, BIRMINGHAM

182 Broad Street, B15 1DA / Tel. 0121 633 1520
www.theworksbirmingham.com

"The best clubbing experience in the UK", though they don't allow sportswear so our footballers will have to get changed before their post-match celebrations.

Tabloid tales

Jermaine Pennant was thrown out for being drunk in February 2006, after a Kanye West concert at which two bouncers were shot (by someone else, we should add). "I just have to be more clever," the winger said, astutely.

THE WORLD CUP

England beat Hungary 3-1 in the first of two warm-up matches ... Peter Crouch sparks new dance craze with what he terms the "robokop", Steven Gerrard comes over all Cristiano Ronaldo when tumbling in the box to "earn" England a penalty ... Sol Campbell's ex-girlfriend Kelly Hoppen reveals the England reserve is obsessed with the Weather Channel ... Boy of '66 George Cohen is unimpressed at the selection of Owen Hargreaves, asking "Can anyone tell me why he's even there?" ... Andriy Shevchenko joins Chelsea for £30million ... Michael Owen admits to a strange pre-match ritual: "I put my right boot and my right shin pad on first. Then I'll probably go for three or four wees". Way too much detail, Michael ... David Beckham is mobbed by 1,000 fans on a Manchester shopping trip. Not 998 or 1,006 but exactly a thousand. Spooky ... Sven-Goran Eriksson vows to do a "robokop" if England win the World Cup. You're safe there then, son ... Crouch scores hat-trick in friendly win over Jamaica ... "Our dressing room was like an episode of MASH," says Dutch boss Marco van Basten after a bruising friendly against Australia ... England's World Cup supplies include 24 cans of styling mousse, 24 vibrating razors and 1,600 jaffa cakes. Each player also has their own wide screen TV complete with Skybox ... Subbuteo announce plans to release a dancing Peter Crouch figure ... Fifty per cent of English workers plan to skive during the World Cup compared with a global average of 26% ... England players' bonus for winning the World Cup is said to be £300,000 each. Expensive peanuts, yes, but peanuts all the same ... England's representatives at the World Cup opening gala concert are Right Said Fred ... Wayne Rooney takes round-trip from Baden-Baden to Manchester to be given all-clear on metatarsal injury ... In the Ukraine a man strangles his wife because she kept talking throughout a televised match ... Doctors warn that new football boots can cause toxic shock syndrome ... WAGs arrive in Germany apart from Lampard's fiancée Elen Rivas who missed her flight after a row about hand luggage ... Brazil's president Luiz Inacio Lula Da Silva pulls no punches in a link up with the squad, asking boss Carlos Alberto Parreirra, "Is Ronaldo really fat?" ... Ecuador coach Luis Fernando Suarez imposes sex ban ... England beat Paraguay 1-0 ... Coldplay singer Chris Martin reveals he's writing an ode to Peter Crouch. The unlistenable in pursuit of the unwatchable ... Cristiano Ronaldo refuses to autograph a fan's breast ... "If we were to beat England, Trinidad & Tobago would close down for a week," says Carlos Edwards ... England beat Trinidad 2-0 ... Ivory Coast players splash out over £14,000 in one electrical shop after being given an afternoon off ... "I nearly signed Shevchenko when I was at West Ham but Lee Chapman was playing well at the time," quips Harry Redknapp... Lionel Messi has "La Mano de Dios" (Hand of God) embroidered on his boots ... England draw 2-2 with Sweden ... WAGs in nightclub bust up. Cheryl and Victoria leave the band to become a double act WAGs Platinum. An unnamed relative begins a 2am chorus of "Ten German bombers" ... Ecuadorian witch doctor places a spell on the England team ... Flavio wins a £100,000 house after scoring Angola's first and only goal in the World Cup ... "I'm not married to David Beckham," reveals Sven ... Baboons at Knowsley Safari Park building up a collection of England flags stolen from visiting cars ... "Wayne Rooney wants to spar with me for the belt but I'm not sure it will fit round his waist," says City fan Ricky Hatton in trash talk epic ... Graham Poll plays his three-card trick during Croatia v Australia and wins himself a one-way ticket to Tring ... WAGs spend £2,000 on champagne and cigarettes in Garibaldi's bar in Baden-Baden ... England beat Ecuador 1-0 and David Beckham is sick on the pitch after scoring the winner ... Eric Abidal tempers the tension of the knockout phase with a sobering insight: "It's kill or be killed. Not literally, of course, as you can't kill with a ball" ... George Cohen's England shirt sells for £38,400 at auction (presumably not bought by Owen Hargreaves) ... Seventy thousand England fans drank 1.2m pints in Nuremburg ... "It's all about winning - not how you do it," says Steve McClaren. Inspiring stuff ... Sven's agent hawks round his autobiography, looking for an advance of £1.5m. First half will be good. Second half, not so good ... Posh and Gabby Logan return to England for emergency treatment on their hair. But only one of them writes a 1,000 word column on the subject and she's married to a rugby player... A punter/fool stakes £200,000 in cash on England to win the World Cup ... Paris Hilton announces German wunderkind Lucas Podolski has taken her fancy ...The owner of Garibaldi's unsurprisingly enjoys having the WAGs' money, sorry, company. "I don't mind them dancing on the tables. Their stilettos haven't left any scratches," he says ... A best man advertises on eBay for someone to take over his duties as they clash with England's quarter-final ... Argentina's players lose with grace, starring in a 34-man brawl after their penalty defeat ... The World Cup's Russell Grant, Raymond Domenech, claims "it was written in the stars that we'd beat Spain" ... England crash out in all too predictable style ... Rooney threatens to "split Ronaldo in two" and the WAGs are taunted by Portuguese WAGs. Much weeping ensues ... "The Holy Father is always impartial," says a Vatican spokesman. OK, perhaps for Germany v Italy but what about good v evil? ... Racehorse owner Gary Martin has his colt "Ronaldo" gelded ... Rio Ferdinand admits he's embarrassed to go out after the latest World Cup disappointment. Oh come on, the wind-up programme wasn't that bad ... "Footballers' wives have no careers and live off their husbands' money," says Cheryl Tweedy, who at least takes her own credit card shopping with her just in case there's a problem with Ashley's ... "I will never understand why Rooney was abandoned up front," says Pele ... A statue of Ronaldinho is torched in Rio after Brazil's early exit ... Zinedine Zidane beats Homer Simpson to the coveted crown of "The greatest ever bald man" but then gets sent off in the World Cup Final ... Italy win the World Cup and Mauro Camoranesi has the pony-tail he's grown for four years cut off by his colleagues as they wait to be given the trophy ...

WORLD CUP

THE GROUPS

Group A

Winners: **Germany** Runners-up: **Ecuador**

Memorable match: **Germany 4 Costa Rica 2**

Hosts go goal crazy in the opening game, with long-range strikes from Frings and Lahm prompting pundits to point at the balls and predict many similar supergoals. It didn't happen.

Group B

Winners: **England** Runners-up: **Sweden**

Memorable match: **England 2 Sweden 2**

Joe Cole scored a goal good enough to prove that England might, after all, have the skills to win the World Cup; Henrik Larsson scored one bad enough to prove they weren't.

Group C

Winners: **Argentina** Runners-up: **Holland**

Memorable match:

Argentina 6 Serbia & Montenegro 0

S&M conceded just one goal in their entire qualifying campaign, presumably because they were saving up all their dodgy defending for a single afternoon in Gelsenkirchen. Cambiasso scored the best goal ever. Really.

Group D

Winners: **Portugal** Runners-up: **Mexico**

Memorable match: **Angola 0 Portugal 1**

In the World Cup's most boring group, this match between African debutants and their former colonial masters at least promised some needle. It didn't deliver, and the most remarkable thing about it was that Pauleta scored.

Group E

Winners: **Italy** Runners-up: **Ghana**

Memorable match: **Czech Republic 0 Ghana 2**

The biggest shock of the first round saw Ghana score two, and miss at least a hundred further chances, against the highly-fancied, though not for long, Czechs.

Group F

Winners: **Brazil** Runners-up: **Australia**

Memorable match: **Australia 3 Japan 1**

In which Tim Cahill came off the bench to rescue the game for Australia, whose three goals came in the last six minutes. Japan should have had a penalty after Australia's equaliser, a fact the Australians conveniently forgot when they had their own penalty misery in due course.

Group G

Winners: **Switzerland** Runners-up: **France**

Memorable match: **France 1 South Korea 1**

France's second game and second draw, and the moment the world realised that they were rubbish, were full of past-it players living off their reputations and would get knocked out really soon.

Group H

Winners: **Spain** Runners-up: **Ukraine**

Memorable match: **Spain 4 Ukraine 0**

Spain start their tournament with a wildly impressive thrashing. Little did they know that they would be on a plane home before their humiliated opponents, who didn't concede again until the quarter-finals.

THE KNOCK OUT ROUND

Germany 2 Sweden 0

Swedes fail to recover from Germany's early blitz. Not sure that's a very apt use of the word blitz, but there you go.

Argentina 2 Mexico 1 (aet)

Two early goals and one very late one, the last one – a chest down and dipping volley by Maxi Rodriguez – was the best by far.

Italy 1 Australia 0

Italy claim fortunate stoppage-time penalty as humiliation beckons. Totti knocks it in, the only decent thing he did all tournament.

Switzerland 0 Ukraine 0
(Ukraine win 3-0 on penalties)
Switzerland, a team even more boring than the nation they represent, didn't concede a single goal in Germany but couldn't score a single penalty either.

England 1 Ecuador 0
David Beckham's free-kick enlivens the dullest display by England in a knock-out event ever. Probably.

Portugal 1 Holland 0
Rampant cheating from both sides, but Portugal are a bit better at it. And at scoring goals, too.

Brazil 3 Ghana 0
Brazil get a pummelling but can't score. Surprisingly both Ronaldo and Adriano do, though one is fat and the other is offside. And fat.

Spain 1 France 3
David Villa puts Spain ahead, proving how rubbish France are. France then score three times. What are the odds?

THE QUARTER-FINALS

Germany 1 Argentina 1
(Germany win 4-2 on penalties)
Argentina score, are so comfortable they take off their best players and don't even bring on their best substitutes. Then they lose.

Italy 3 Ukraine 0
Hang one, what are Ukraine still doing here? Will someone knock them out please, they're rubbish. Thank you.

England 0 Portugal 0
(Portugal win 3-1 on penalties)
The referee complies with Cristiano Ronaldo's polite request for him to send Wayne Rooney off for no reason and England are out. On penalties, inevitably.

Brazil 0 France 1
In which Zinedine Zidane proved that he was still a genius. This revelation will go down as his penultimate great surprise of the tournament.

THE SEMI-FINALS

Germany 0 Italy 2 (aet)
Quite a dull game but a brilliant extra-time ends with two Italy goals in the last two minutes and the hosts are, as they say, aus.

Portugal 0 France 1
Thierry Henry wins a penalty, Zidane scores it and France are in the final. Portugal are robbed by referee who fails to award Cristiano Ronaldo the penalty he politely requested.

THE 3RD & 4TH PLACE

Germany 3 Portugal 1
Nobody cares about this match except the team that wins it. Bastian Schweinsteiger scored a couple of good goals. His name means pig-climber, by the way.

THE FINAL

Italy 1 France 1 (Italy win 5-3 on penalties)
With 10 minutes of extra time remaining Zinedine Zidane, realising he'd been involved in a boring final and feeling personally responsible, headbutts Marco Materazzi. Referee Horacio Elizondo, having already sent off Wayne Rooney, continues his one-man campaign against European talent, and the rest of the world gets at least one decent memory from the so-called showpiece.

WORLD CUP

BIG PHIL SCOLARI'S
Dossier
+ + + + + + + May 2006 + + + + + + +

Brian Barwick — oso nova....

arrogante
imenso grande
enorme volumoso gravida
importante
"BIG" Felipe Scolari

I am officially now the owner of a short, balding, bespectacled, politely exasperated, philosophically retrograde, conservative Swedish gentleman. Those are the rules of this game – win three times and you get to take him home with you to keep. Now, where shall I put him, Olga, perhaps the cupboard under the stairs?

It's ironic I suppose that they wanted me to go into the quarter-final with divided loyalties as England manager elect. But Big Phil is a loyal man. When I spoke to the Englishmen they told me of their vision for the future. "Look at us, our PR is all over the place," said Barwickao. "The press hate the manager. They say he is impervious to criticism, that we play negatively, wasted a golden generation, sticks rigidly to a 4-5-1 that the players, fans and press despise, have players who go down too easily in the penalty area, hasn't got a clue about how to use substitutes to change the course of a game, indulges an over-the-hill galactico captain and blames everyone but himself. We need to change."

"Well, I know how to make substitutions," I said, and he made a big green tick on the back of an envelope as Brookinginho beamed at me and said, "When can you start?" But it wasn't to be. They pushed me for a quick answer, to betray my word and honour to the alma mater of my mother tongue. But I am a man and men do not do such things. So, I plotted my revenge against these dishonourable half-men with their national newspapers and their lookalike obsession that wanted me to spend the next two years saying, "No, I am not bloody Gene Hackman" every day but won't wait a month for me.

After a quick tune-up against Holland, my men were ready for the English. I asked them once again to stand up to be counted as men, and in Ricardo Carvalho, a real man who laid down his testicles for his colleagues, we had a true warrior infused with the spirit of the battle. Off went Wayne Rooney after his penis polka and the game was ours. All we had to do was wait for penalties for the men to leave the boys behind. And just as I knew we would, we won. Why did we win? The English press tried to blame Cristiano Ronaldo for his "Hello, cheeky" wink but that was not directed at me but at a woman in the crowd because he is a man, a winner and irresistible to women.

No, we won because we can punch our hearts with our fists without flinching, we have iron in our scrotums, we smell musky, we have adam's apples and stubby masculine fingers.

We won because we are men and men win.

Olga, bring meat.

A FIRST XI OF WORLD CUP EXCUSES
(LESS A SENDING OFF, OF COURSE)

1 THE HEAT

Everyone knows football is best played in the cold, when players can run for 90 minutes without worrying about sunstroke or dehydration, and the only reason for the ground to be uncomfortably hard is that it's been frozen solid. But it also helps to have unblemished pitches, of the sort that can only be maintained when there isn't too much rain and players don't run all over it all the time. It needs summer pitches but winter conditions.

Sample quote: "I'm not worried we faded. Our performance was totally down to the heat." – David Beckham

2 DEHYDRATION

You can't really point the finger at any individual for it being hot, but if you're not allowed to drink when you're thirsty it's a different story. It is always easier to blame someone who you know exists though you wish he didn't, like the Fifa chief Sepp Blatter who was responsible for the brief water ban, than someone who might not exist though you wish he did, like God, who was responsible for the heat.

Sample quote: "There was a couple of times when you went over to try and get a drink, and for some reason they didn't want us to." – Joe Cole

3 THE REFEREES

Always a common cause of complaint. Of all the things they got wrong, their handling of Portugal in the World Cup was the worst – the Portuguese were furious that they weren't awarded lots of penalties, their opponents that the Iberians' ludicrous diving to win highly dubious penalties had gone unpunished.

Sample quote: "Everyone could see the referee wasn't fair. He should have shown many yellow cards to their players but he did not do that because Portugal is a small country and France is a big one." – Cristiano Ronaldo

4 ILLNESS

This is the one Ronaldo wheels out when he does badly. At the 1998 World Cup final he played like a lame donkey with its legs strapped together, and then news came out that he had suffered a mysterious fit. In 2006 he meandered through Brazil's first game against Croatia as if drugged, blindfolded, spun round in a circle 15 times and then forced to parade through the central square of a major capital city naked, and promptly complained of "dizziness".

Sample quote: "I felt sick and the doctor took me to the hospital for a series of examinations. There was nothing abnormal ... I'm feeling much better today." – Ronaldo

NATIONAL CHARACTERISTICS

5 The ultimate excuse, suggesting that your team's performance is genetically predetermined. Frequently used when people lose to African nations, who are cursed with being "better suited to these conditions", or when a team is about to face either Brazil or any Caribbean nation, who inevitably "play with a smile on their face" and "know how to party". In 2006 the Italy maestro Marcello Lippi blamed his nation for the fact that Daniele De Rossi was sent off for viciously elbowing Brian McBride for no apparent reason.

Sample quote: "Unfortunately, Italian players have these habits and they have a tough time at the international level." – Marcello Lippi

FROGS

6 Extra marks for originality go to Ukraine, who blamed their 4-0 thrashing by Spain in their opening Group H encounter on the frogs that frolic in the lake by their hotel in Potsdam.

Sample quote: "We can barely sleep at night because of the croaking. We have agreed we will take fishing rods to hunt these frogs." – Vladislav Vashchyuk

OTHER PEOPLE

7 Ask a player why his team has failed and there are a million possible answers, all of which could be summed up under this heading. The player himself, clearly, is not to blame.

Sample quote: "In my position I'm reliant on the team doing better. If I get chances I'll score goals." – Michael Owen

FIGHTING

8 The pressure-cooker atmosphere that builds up during a month or more spent together as a squad can result in players turning on each other.

Sample quote: "We are very passionate and want Sweden to do our best. We didn't win and we just discussed how we can do better next time. There was no fight."
– Freddie Ljungberg, after his, er, "discussion" with Olof Mellberg

THE PITCH

9 An all-time classic excuse. Ruud van Nistelrooy merrily alleged that "the playing field was so rough it made me stumble over the ball", although the truth of the matter was clearly that he was out of form and being a bit clumsy.

Sample quote: "The conditions have made it hard for us. They are not watering the pitches. It is slowing our passing game down." – Paul Robinson

THE BALL

10 A favourite among goalkeepers. As the American coach Bruce Arena said after his own goalkeeper spoke out against the latest adidas effort: "The goalkeepers don't like this ball and they didn't like the ball four years ago. Let's face it, they never like the ball."

Sample quote: "These balls are definitely not goalkeeper friendly. It is a very light, fast ball. It moves quicker in the air. Not only that, it has a wobble." – Kasey Keller

WORLD CUP
Balls

World Cup skill school

Emulate your heroes from the World Cup and humiliate your friends by learning the skills that helped these top internationals grab the attention of the entire galaxy in Germany last summer.

1. **Argentina's team goal against Serbia**
   a. Assemble a group of friends. Note that all of them should be quite good at football
   b. Find a group of children no older than 11, and at least four years younger than you
   c. Tell them you'll hurt them if they tackle you
   d. Pass the ball among yourselves at will
   e. Voila!

2. **Joe Cole's dipping volley**
   a. Find a short goalkeeper. Blindfold him
   b. Throw the ball into the air, and position yourself so that it will land on your chest.
   c. The ball drops towards your foot
   d. Volley it gracefully past the hopeless keeper. If you get it wrong, remember that the goalkeeper is blindfolded, so you can tell him that you got it right
   e. Voila!

3. **Wayne Rooney's stamp**
   Not for the faint-hearted.
   a. Break foot
   b. Wear large medical boot for a couple of weeks and sleep in an oxygen tent
   c. Declare fitness
   d. Run around stamping on things. If you run out of things, stamp on people. Continue until shouted at.
   e. Voila!

Waah! Those wannabe Argie twats won't give me a go

4. **The Ronaldo fall**
   This extra-special skill has the added advantage of being one you can practice on your own.
   a. Run at pace with a football tied to your feet
   b. Jump
   c. While in mid-air, try to turn 180 degrees and, at the point of landing, shoot an imploring glance at the referee (who can be imaginary, if necessary)
   d. Put your head in your hands when the imaginary referee ignores you
   e. Voila!

5. **Zinedine Zidane's butt**
   The only fitting way to remember a player of such varied skills is, of course, by headbutting your friends at every available opportunity.
   a. Find a friend
   b. Engage in friendly, relaxed conversation
   c. Go for a stroll if you like. Keep talking
   d. Headbutt them viciously in the chest. Accuse them of saying something "serious"
   e. Voila!

Mon Dieu, Zizou!

Balls! has asked the world's leading experts in violence, scar-faced nutters in satin bomber jackets with a propensity to scream "no fucking trainers, granddad", to account for the French captain's actions which led to his red card in the Final. Here are the results:

1. Being preoccupied with the letter "Z", Zidane wanted to patent a new martial arts move to paralyse the larynx and to call it the "zed-butt".

2. He wanted to leave a perfect impression of the world's best footballer's face in the form of a livid bruise to complement Materazzi's array of tattoos.

3. Incensed by his half-time perusal of Asterix the Gladiator, he recognises a lieneage all the way back to the fiendish Odius Asparagus in Materazzi's aquiline hooter.

4. Roused by the pre-match bellowing of the Marseillaise, he took the imprecation,

   "Citizens take up arms
   Form your battalions
   March, march
   Spill the enemy's blood
   Over the land"
   a smidgeon too literally.

5. Zidane's four sons' favourite book is *The Three Billy Goats Gruff* and their father was merely enacting the famous scene when an ugly troll was blocking the hero's passage.

6. Temporarily possessed by the spirit of a famished, rogue rhinoceros trying to dislodge a bucket of carrots impaled on his horn during excessively hasty nosh up.

7. It was nothing more than an incredibly violent sneeze with such a nose-tingling build-up it necessitated three steps forward before the frantic search for somewhere to wipe.

8. Knowing that Zinédine in Arabic means "ornament of the faith" and Zidane means "increases the faith", Materazzi adopts high-pitched, sarcastic voice to wail George Michael's theme song one too many times while dancing around imaginary handbag.

9. Materazzi had been in contact with his Goodison Park connections and uttered the most chilling words a world-class footballer can hear: "David Moyes is interested in you ..."

10. Because Materazzi deserved it.

Graham Poll

I booked him how many times? You're having a laugh!

Date of birth: 29 July 1963
Height: 6ft
Weight: 13st 12lb
Interests: Travelling, reading
Residence: Tring
Nickname: The Thing from Tring
No. of World Cups officiated: 2
No. of World Cups officiated which have not ended with him being sent home in disgrace and humiliation: 0
No. of referees in Benin better than him, judged by appointments to major international matches: 1
No. of referees in England better than him, judged by appointments to major international matches: 0
Marks out of 10: Knowledge of the rules 8; Communication with players 9; Decision-making 8; Forgetting it all as soon as the heat is on 9.

His World Cup in quotes

Poll looks ahead: "If you make a big mistake it will be your last game, and that's something that has been made very clear to us."

Poll looks back: "I realise I made an error in not sending off Josip Simunic. I regret and apologise for this mistake and realise that my World Cup is now over."

Simunic explains: "I think he got all mixed up about me and Dario Simic who also got sent off. But you'd think someone would have spotted it."

Fifa's referee chief Angel Maria Villa Llona (four names, natch) adds: "He made a mistake and he has explained it. He is a man of extraordinary experience. He is a great referee."

Poll continues: "I've been inundated with messages. I had a personal call from Sepp Blatter to urge me to continue. It touches you when the president of Fifa takes trouble to say that you're not rubbish."

Fifa's statement reads: "Graham Poll is an exceptional referee and a great sportsman, who will be able to overcome the situation thanks to his strong personality and love of the game."

Australia captain Mark Viduka surmises: "Everybody makes mistakes. Graham Poll is a top-quality ref. I will not say anything against him."

WORLD CUP

Balls

154

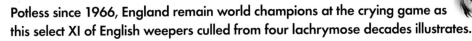

Potless since 1966, England remain world champions at the crying game as this select XI of English weepers culled from four lachrymose decades illustrates.

1. **Sir Bobby Charlton 1966** In floods of tears (but of joy) at the end of extra-time before the "Boys of 66" strode up to receive the Jules Rimet trophy from the Queen.

2. **Paul Gascoigne 1990** Received his second yellow card of the tournament in extra-time of the semi-final and began to howl. Inspired Gary Lineker's famous "Have a word with him" finger-to-eyeball gesture at the bench.

3. **Stuart Pearce 1990** In the penalty shootout Pearce had his weak shot saved by Illgner. Squatted in the centre-circle with a towel draped over his shoulders and his thumb and forefinger as an improvised mask. Redemption came later.

4. **Chris Waddle 1990** Standing in for the distraught Gascoigne, his penalty was struck so sweetly yet with such elevation that an urban myth claims that the ball's arc could be traced only by satellite.

5. **Gareth Southgate 1996** England's sixth penalty in the Euro 96 semi-final was more of a back-pass than a shot. Adopted the knees-up, bum to the floor pose favoured by snake charmers as captured by illustrators of Kipling's stories.

6. **Paul Ince 1998** The first to miss for England v Argentina in the second round. Though David Batty missed the headline-grabbing fifth penalty, his bottom lip wobbled but tears never came. The Guv'nor, however, cried like a baby.

7. **David Seaman 2002** The thirty-eight-year old pony-tailed Yorkshireman blamed himself for Ronaldinho's cross/chip winner as he proved yet again that running backwards is a young man's game.

8. **Darius Vassell 2004** One of the strangest of all international careers. Came from nowhere, no one knew why. Substitute for the injured Rooney in the quarter-final against Portugal, missed England's seventh penalty.

9. **David Beckham 2006** The captain's injury early in the second-half of the quarter-final sent him into a brief paroxysm of self-pity at the prospect of missing leading England in the final. Yes, they really were that deluded.

10. **Rio Ferdinand 2006** Courted nemesis after his hubristic World Cup Wind-ups TV show and the gods duly used him for their sport as he was left covering his gently leaking eyes.

11. **John Terry 2006** Were his uncharacteristic slumped shoulders and bitter tears provoked by rage, sorrow or by the prospect of having to face arch Portuguese patriot Jose Mourinho in three weeks' time?

WORLD CUP
Balls

2010 World Cup guide

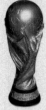

There's only one thing to do after a World Cup ends – start looking forward to the next one. In 2010, the eyes of the world will be focused on South Africa, the first time that the premier international footballing event will have been held outside its traditional heartlands of Europe, South America, North America, Central America and Asia.

There will be plenty of time for more complete guides to the event over the next three and a bit years but to get the ball rolling here's the vital information about each ground: what it's called, how many people it holds, and how likely you are to be eaten by either a lion or a shark on your way to the game.

1. **NELSON MANDELA BAY STADIUM, PORT ELIZABETH**
   Capacity: 50,000

   Boasts 40km of "immaculate" beaches with Pollock Beach, known as The Pipe, a favourite for surfers – the great white's snack of choice. Also offers "close proximity" to game reserves.

   SHARK RATING: 5/5 **LION RATING** 3/5

2. **MBOMBELA STADIUM, NELSPRUIT**
   Capacity: 40,000

   Nelspruit is the gateway to the Great Limpopo Transfrontier Park, which means that you will never be far from a giraffe. The sea isn't far away either, but there are no beaches immediately to hand.

   SHARK RATING: 1/5 **LION RATING** 5/5

3. **GREENPOINT STADIUM, CAPE TOWN**
   (also known as the African Renaissance Stadium)
   Capacity: 68,000

   Nowhere near any game reserves but offers plenty of beaches and excellent whale watching. If you do fall prey to a great white, don't try to visit the local Cape Doctor, which is not a doctor at all but in fact a wind.

   SHARK RATING: 4/5 **LION RATING:** 0/5

4. **KING'S PARK STADIUM, DURBAN**
   (also the King Senzangakhona Stadium)
   Capacity: 60,000

   Africa's busiest port offers "exquisite" beaches running down the KwaZulu Natal coast. Plenty of birdlife, but not many great predators. England beat South Africa 2-1 here in 2003.

   SHARK RATING 4/5 **LION RATING** 1/5

5. **ROYAL BAFOKENG SPORTS PALACE, RUSTENBURG**
   Capacity: 40,000

   Lying well inland, this is the world's platinum capital and is handy for seven (count 'em) national parks for your big game needs. The stadium, sorry "sports palace", is owned by the indigenous Bafokeng tribe.

   SHARK RATING 0/5 **LION RATING** 4/5

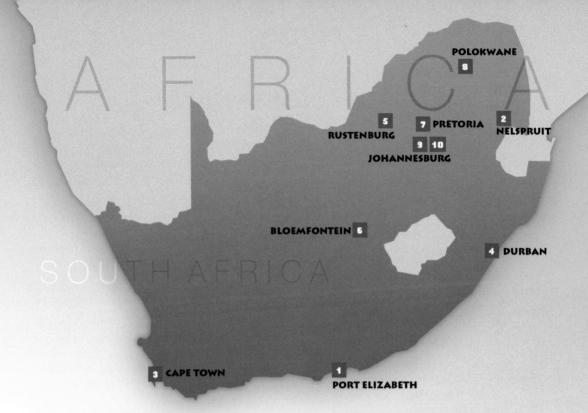

POLOKWANE
8

5   **7** PRETORIA   **2**
RUSTENBURG   NELSPRUIT
9 10
JOHANNESBURG

BLOEMFONTEIN **6**

4 DURBAN

SOUTH AFRICA

3 CAPE TOWN   **1**
PORT ELIZABETH

6. FREE STATE STADIUM, BLOEMFONTEIN
Capacity: 40,000

Part of the Mangaung Metroploitan, mangaung being Sotho for "place where cheetahs dwell", though the city was named after the flowers that bloom here in the picturesque springtime. The stadium was originally built in 1952. Emphatically landlocked.

SHARK RATING 0/5   LION RATING 2/5   CHEETAH RATING 5/5

7. LOFTUS VERSFELD STADIUM, PRETORIA
Capacity: 52,000

The country's administrative capital is part of the Tshwane Metropolitan Municipality, tshwane meaning "little ape" in Ndebele. Swimmers note: the only seas you'll see here are embassies (geddit?).

SHARK RATING: 0/5   LION RATING: 1/5   LITTLE APE RATING: 5/5

8. PETER MOKABA STADIUM, POLOKWANE
Capacity: 40,000

Another landlocked town, this is the traditional home of the rain queen, Modjadji the Fifth, which is an entertaining way of telling the prospective visitor to pack an umbrella. On the predator front, Kruger National Park is not far away.

SHARK RATING: 0/5   LION RATING: 2/5   RAIN RATING: 5/5

9. SOCCER CITY, JOHANNESBURG
Capacity: 94,700

10. ELLIS PARK STADIUM, JOHANNESBURG
Capacity: 60,000

Just as far from the sea as any of the other places we've already said are a long way from the sea, 40% of the world's gold comes from this area, and the same proportion of South Africa's population lives nearby. They tend to scare off the lions, frankly.

SHARK RATING: 0/5   LION RATING: 0/5

WORLD CUP

Balls

157

Balls Beckham's Homework

In March the England captain David Beckham complained that he was unable to make sense of his seven-year-old son's maths homework. "It's so hard these days," he said. "I sat down with Brooklyn the other day and I was so like, 'Victoria, maybe you should do the homework tonight.' It's totally different to what I was taught when I was at school. I was like, 'Oh my God, I can't do this.'"

Well, David, here at **Balls!** Academy we pride ourselves on having taught you well. See if you can have a go at this exam on all what you have been learnt without recourse to Victoria's hidden academic talents.

Section 1: General knowledge

1. In football, how far from goal is the penalty spot?
   - [ ] a) 10 yards
   - [ ] b) 12 yards
   - [ ] c) 18 yards
   - [ ] d) too far

2. Who is going to host the next football World Cup in 2010?
   - [ ] a) Brazil
   - [ ] b) China
   - [ ] c) Australia
   - [ ] d) South Africa

3. Who did Tony Blair support as a child?
   - [ ] a) Manchester United
   - [ ] b) Newcastle United
   - [ ] c) Torquay United
   - [ ] d) Sheffield United

4. Who plays at Sincil Bank?
   - [ ] a) Lincoln
   - [ ] b) Liverpool
   - [ ] c) Luton
   - [ ] d) Real Madrid

5. Who is the chairman of Portsmouth?
   - [ ] a) Sergei Guidemback
   - [ ] b) Sacha Gaydamak
   - [ ] c) Serhiy Gastromov
   - [ ] d) Doug Ellis

Section 2: Appearance

1. According to a recent poll, how many footballers in the entire history of the game have been sexier that Ray "Butch" Wilkins?
   - [ ] a) 13
   - [ ] b) 130
   - [ ] c) 1,300
   - [ ] d) my calculator's broken

2. In October, TV presenter Paul O'Grady advised Wayne Rooney's fiancée Coleen McLoughlin to get a:
   - [ ] a) haircut
   - [ ] b) new outfit
   - [ ] c) new boyfriend
   - [ ] d) job

3. Permanently-injured midfielder David Dunn will, he admits, always have a big what?
   - [ ] a) house
   - [ ] b) car
   - [ ] c) bank account
   - [ ] d) arse

4. What would typically appear on a pair of Djibril Cisse's underwear?
   - [ ] a) stripes
   - [ ] b) stars
   - [ ] c) zebra print
   - [ ] d) streak marks

5. Which company holds the Beckham warrant for the supply of skiwear?
   - [ ] a) Snow & Rock
   - [ ] b) El Cortes Ingles
   - [ ] c) Milletts
   - [ ] d) Chanel

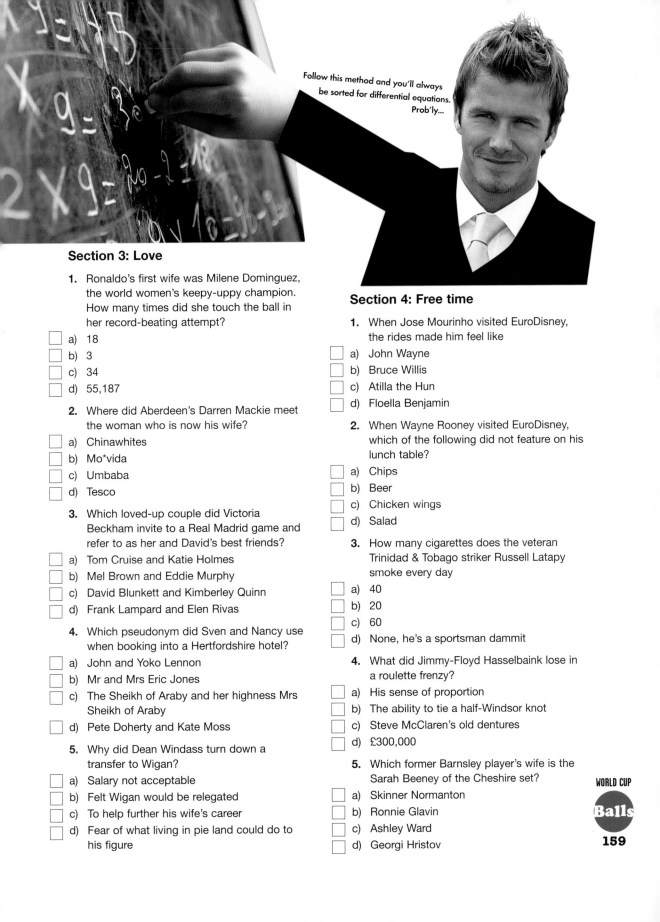

Follow this method and you'll always be sorted for differential equations. Prob'ly...

Section 3: Love

1. Ronaldo's first wife was Milene Dominguez, the world women's keepy-uppy champion. How many times did she touch the ball in her record-beating attempt?

- [ ] a) 18
- [ ] b) 3
- [ ] c) 34
- [ ] d) 55,187

2. Where did Aberdeen's Darren Mackie meet the woman who is now his wife?

- [ ] a) Chinawhites
- [ ] b) Mo*vida
- [ ] c) Umbaba
- [ ] d) Tesco

3. Which loved-up couple did Victoria Beckham invite to a Real Madrid game and refer to as her and David's best friends?

- [ ] a) Tom Cruise and Katie Holmes
- [ ] b) Mel Brown and Eddie Murphy
- [ ] c) David Blunkett and Kimberley Quinn
- [ ] d) Frank Lampard and Elen Rivas

4. Which pseudonym did Sven and Nancy use when booking into a Hertfordshire hotel?

- [ ] a) John and Yoko Lennon
- [ ] b) Mr and Mrs Eric Jones
- [ ] c) The Sheikh of Araby and her highness Mrs Sheikh of Araby
- [ ] d) Pete Doherty and Kate Moss

5. Why did Dean Windass turn down a transfer to Wigan?

- [ ] a) Salary not acceptable
- [ ] b) Felt Wigan would be relegated
- [ ] c) To help further his wife's career
- [ ] d) Fear of what living in pie land could do to his figure

Section 4: Free time

1. When Jose Mourinho visited EuroDisney, the rides made him feel like

- [ ] a) John Wayne
- [ ] b) Bruce Willis
- [ ] c) Atilla the Hun
- [ ] d) Floella Benjamin

2. When Wayne Rooney visited EuroDisney, which of the following did not feature on his lunch table?

- [ ] a) Chips
- [ ] b) Beer
- [ ] c) Chicken wings
- [ ] d) Salad

3. How many cigarettes does the veteran Trinidad & Tobago striker Russell Latapy smoke every day

- [ ] a) 40
- [ ] b) 20
- [ ] c) 60
- [ ] d) None, he's a sportsman dammit

4. What did Jimmy-Floyd Hasselbaink lose in a roulette frenzy?

- [ ] a) His sense of proportion
- [ ] b) The ability to tie a half-Windsor knot
- [ ] c) Steve McClaren's old dentures
- [ ] d) £300,000

5. Which former Barnsley player's wife is the Sarah Beeney of the Cheshire set?

- [ ] a) Skinner Normanton
- [ ] b) Ronnie Glavin
- [ ] c) Ashley Ward
- [ ] d) Georgi Hristov

Section 5: Lost & found

1. In August, the Chelsea mascot Stamford the Lion was stolen. His head was eventually recovered close to another Premiership ground, but where?

- [ ] a) Newcastle
- [ ] b) Blackburn
- [ ] c) Watford
- [ ] d) Portsmouth

2. In February the Littlewoods Cup was found in the company's offices. But where?

- [ ] a) a storeroom
- [ ] b) a safe
- [ ] c) the canteen
- [ ] d) in the director's excessively large fish tank

3. What did Anton Ferdinand lose outside a kebab shop in September?

- [ ] a) His dignity
- [ ] b) His patience after Rio practised a World Cup prank on his brother involving extra-hot chilli sauce
- [ ] c) His barber's telephone number
- [ ] d) His 10k Rolex, jewellery and mobile

4. What did Mauro Camoranesi lose moments after winning the World Cup?

- [ ] a) Easter Island statue lookalike competition
- [ ] b) Marco Materazzi's application to join the Zinedine Zidane fan club
- [ ] c) His pony-tail
- [ ] d) The will to play for Juventus in Serie B

5. What did Mick Quinn lose and find?

- [ ] a) 4lb 8oz and his feet
- [ ] b) His reality TV show virginity and his bank manager's telephone number
- [ ] c) The will to live and that Anne Diamond cheats
- [ ] d) His roly-poly bonhomie and the ability to beat a 21 stone astrologer in a race.

Answers: Section 1: 1-b; 2-d; 3-b; 4-a; 5-b / **Section 2:** 1-a; 2-d; 3-d; 4-c; 5-d / **Section 3:** 1-d; 2-a; 3-d; 4-b; 3-c
Section 4: 1-b; 2-d; 3-a; 5-c / **Section 5:** 1-c; 2-a; 3-d; 4-c; 5-a

So you see, grasshopper, football is simply a metaphor for life.

On your wedge? Bollocks, is it!